Introduction

Basic Concepts and Skills

Writing Readiness

Reading Readiness

Mathematics Readiness

Appendix

Over 10 Million Copies in Print!

COMPREHENSIVE CURRICULUM of Basic Skills

PRE K

Math Readiness

Reading Readiness

Writing Readiness

Colors, Shapes, and Sizes

Thinking Kids™
Carson-Dellosa Publishing LLC
Greensboro, North Carolina

Thinking Kids™
Carson-Dellosa Publishing LLC
P.O. Box 35665
Greensboro, NC 27425 USA

ISBN 978-1-4838-2408-6
01-046161151

What to Expect from Your 3-Year-Old

Motor Development

Your child . . .

- is strengthening and gaining greater control over the large muscles used for running, jumping, and throwing.
- is developing greater control over the small muscles used for drawing,cutting, buttoning, and zipping.

Social/Emotional Development

Your child . . .

- needs praise and encouragement when learning new things.
- can make simple choices between two things.
- spends a lot of time observing others and his world.

Language Development

Your child . . .

- is using language to express his needs and wants more effectively.
- can speak in short sentences using 4 to 6 words.
- enjoys songs, rhymes, and language play.
- is able to tell simple stories from pictures and books.

Cognitive Development

Your child . . .

- is learning to follow directions.
- can identify colors.
- sees similarities and differences in objects.
- can count concrete objects.

What to Expect from Your 4-Year-Old

Motor Development

Your child . . .

- is gaining ever greater control over her large muscles. Your child can now walk a straight line; hop on one foot; jump over objects 5 to 6 inches high; throw, bounce, and catch a ball easily; run; climb; and skip.
- is developing greater control over his small muscles. She should now be able to cut a straight line, print her name, thread small beads on a string, and form recognizable shapes out of modeling clay.

Social/Emotional Development

Your child . . .

- is willing to try new adventures but needs to be watched carefully because she cannot yet estimate her own abilities.
- has a very active imagination.

Language Development

Your child . . .

- is using language effectively to express her needs and wants.
- can speak in sentences using 6 to 8 words.
- can recognize letters and familiar words.
- may be able to print her own name.
- is asking a lot of questions.
- enjoys sharing information with adults and other children.

Cognitive Development

Your child . . .

- can name 6 to 8 colors and 3 shapes.
- can understand the concepts of number, size, position, and time.
- has a longer attention span and can work for at least 10–15 minutes.

Developmental Skills Checklist

This checklist is designed to help you record and assess your child's progress in the following preschool skills. Write the date beside each skill as your child masters it, writing any other comments you may have about your child's progress. You may also want to add to or adapt this checklist to fit your child's abilities.

Basic Skills

Identifies basic colors ____________________

Identifies simple shapes ____________________

Understands positional concepts:

up/down __________ over/under __________ in/out __________

far/near __________ above/below __________ off/on __________

Reading Readiness

Identifies pictures of objects ____________________

Follows simple directions ____________________

Asks simple questions ____________________

Recites the alphabet ____________________

Identifies uppercase letters ____________________

Identifies lowercase letters ____________________

Listens to stories/poems with interest ____________________

Answers questions about a story ____________________

Repeats songs/poems from memory ____________________

Mathematics Readiness

Rote counts to 10 ______________________

Identifies numbers to 10 ______________________

Uses ordinal numbers first through fifth ______________________

Identifies patterns ______________________

Creates simple patterns ______________________

Recognizes quantitative differences:

big/little __________ more/fewer __________ empty/full __________

short/long __________ tall/short __________

Fine (Small) Motor Skills

Holds pencil correctly __________ Traces slanted lines __________

Colors within lines __________ Traces curves and circles __________

Cuts a line with scissors __________ Traces letters and numbers __________

Traces vertical lines __________ Prints first name __________

Traces horizontal lines __________ Prints letters and numbers __________

Gross (Large) Motor Skills

Runs well without falling __________ Balances on one foot __________

Jumps with two feet __________ Skips, alternating feet __________

Walks backward __________ Catches a ball __________

Hops on one foot __________ Can swing well __________

Draw something else that is **red**.

Now, trace the word **red**.

red

YELLOW

Color the pictures **yellow.**

Draw something else that is **yellow**.

Now, trace the word **yellow**.

yellow

 Name ____________________

BLUE

Color the pictures **blue**.

Draw something else that is **blue**.

Now, trace the word **blue**.

blue

 Name ________________

GREEN

Color the pictures **green**.

Draw something else that is **green**.

Now, trace the word **green**.

green

ORANGE

Color the pictures **orange**.

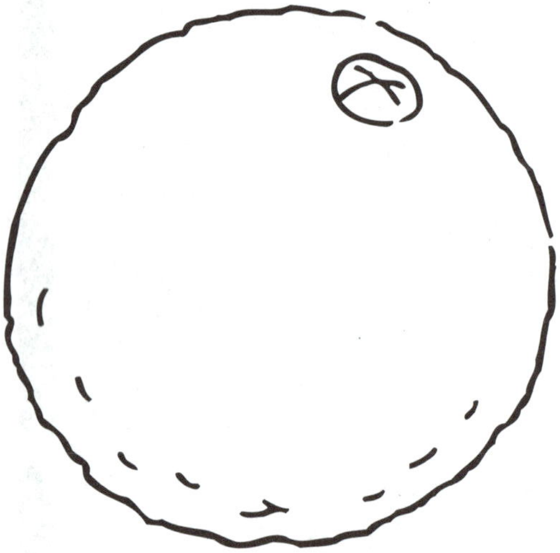

Draw something else that is **orange**.

Now, trace the word **orange**.

orange

 Name ______________________

PINK

Color the pictures **pink**.

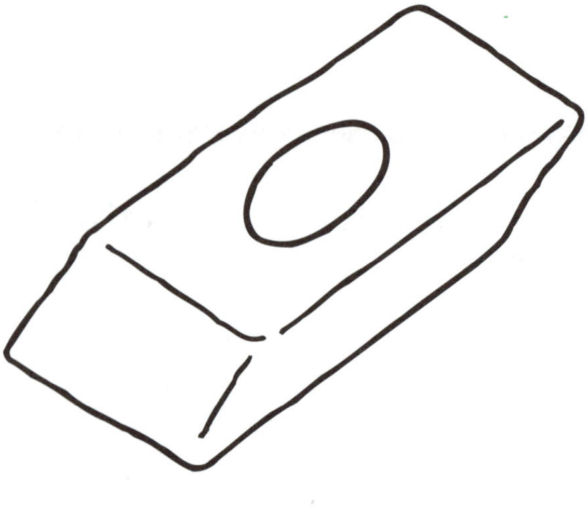

Draw something else that is **pink**.

Now, trace the word **pink**.

pink

 Name ____________________

PURPLE

Color the pictures **purple**.

Draw something else that is **purple**.

Now, trace the word **purple**.

purple

 Name ______________________

BROWN

Color the pictures **brown**.

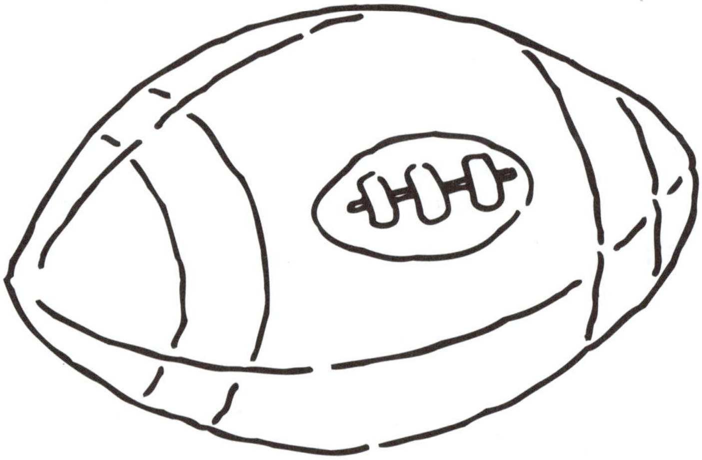

Draw something else that is **brown**.

Now, trace the word **brown**.

brown

BLACK

Color the pictures **black**.

Draw something else that is **black**.

Now, trace the word **black**.

black

 Name ____________________

WHITE

Color the pictures **white**.

Draw something else that is **white**.

Now, trace the word **white**.

white

GRAY

Color the pictures **gray**.

Draw something else that is **gray**.

Now, trace the word **gray**.

gray

Colors

Circle the **red** picture in each row.

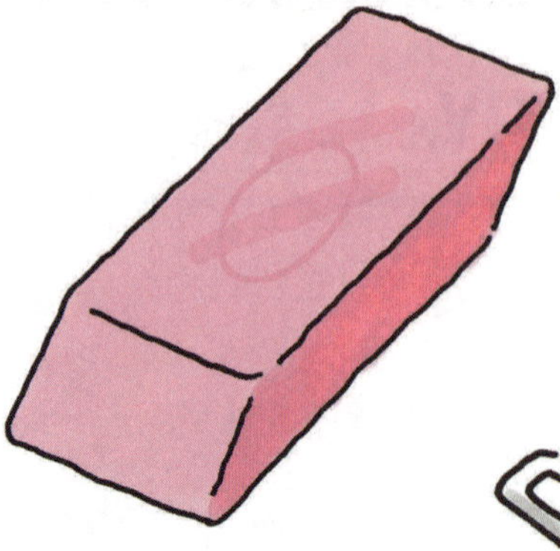

Colors

Circle the **yellow** picture in each row.

 Name ______________________

Colors

Circle the **blue** picture in each row.

Colors

Circle the **green** picture in each row.

 Name ______________________

Colors

Circle the **orange** picture in each row.

Colors

Circle the **pink** picture in each row.

Colors

Circle the **purple** picture in each row.

Colors

Circle the **brown** picture in each row.

Colors

Circle the **black** picture in each row.

Colors

Circle the **white** picture in each row.

 Name ______________________

Colors

Circle the **gray** picture in each row.

Colors

In each row, color two things that are the same color.

 Name ______________________

Colors

In each row, color two things that are the same color.

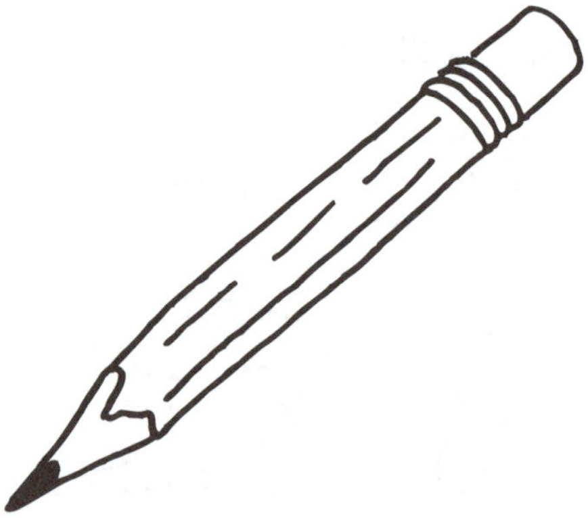

Colors

In each row, color two things that are the same color.

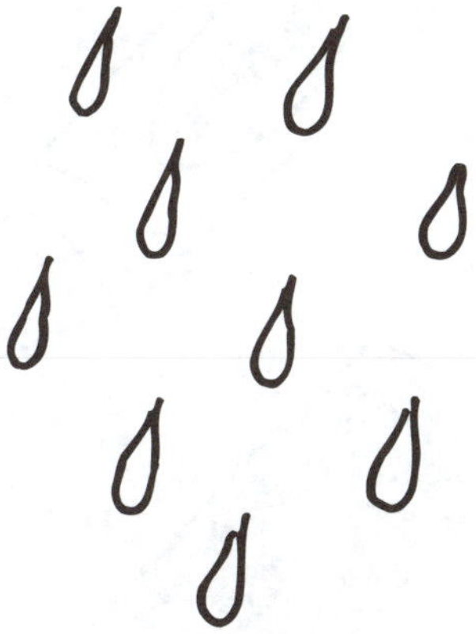

 Name ______________________

Colors

Draw a line to match each picture to the crayon with the same color.

Colors

Draw a line to match each picture to the crayon with the same color.

 Name ____________________

Shapes

This is a **circle**. Trace the shape.

Trace the word.

circle

Shapes

This picture has **circles** in it. Trace the circles.

Shapes

This picture has **circles** in it. Trace the circles.

Shapes

Color the **circles**.

Shapes

This is a **square**. Trace the shape.

Trace the word.

square

Shapes

This picture has **squares** in it. Trace the squares.

Shapes

This picture has **squares** in it. Trace the squares.

Shapes

Color the **squares**.

 Name ______________________

Shapes

This is a **triangle**. Trace the shape.

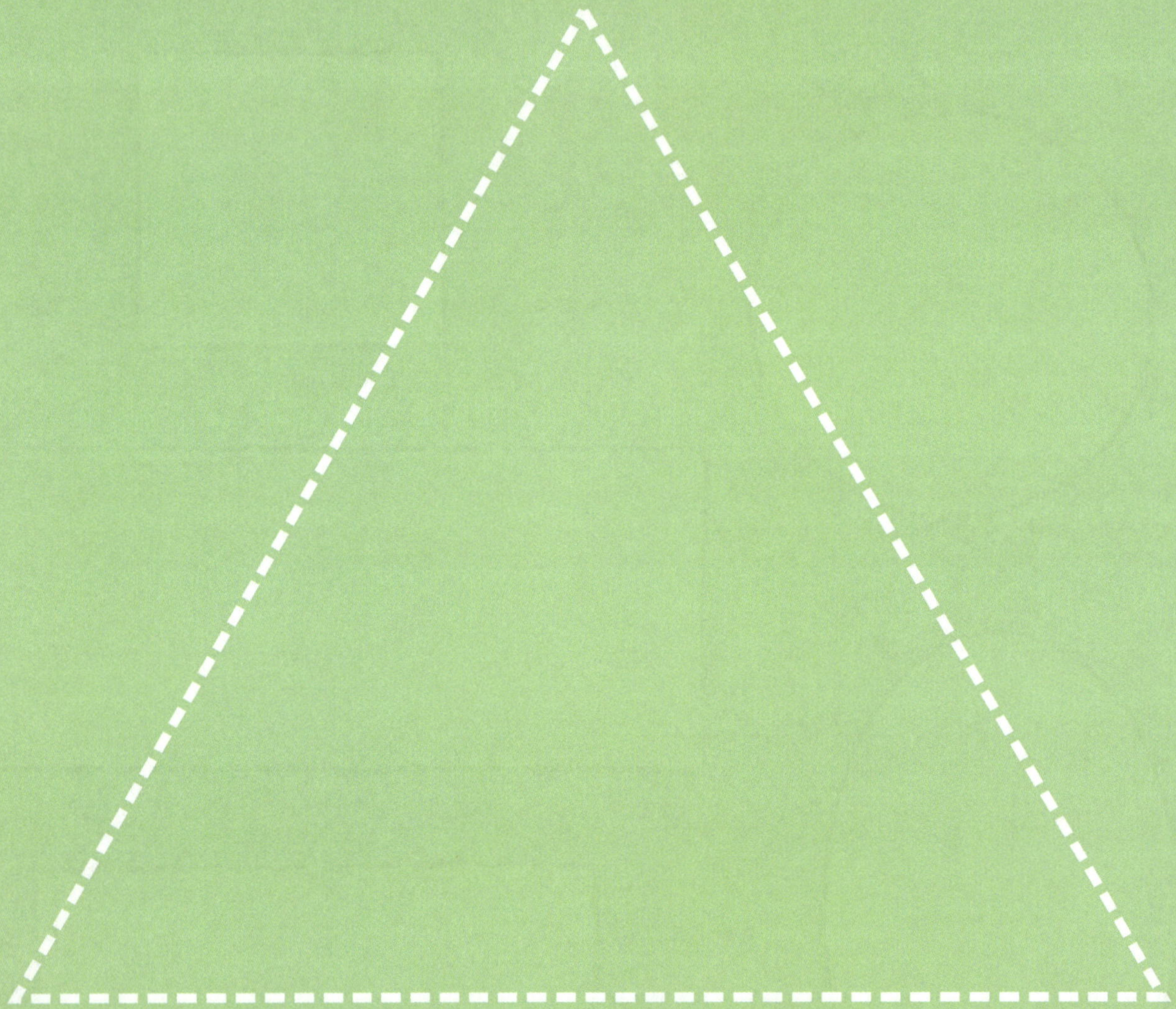

Trace the word.

triangle

Shapes

This picture has **triangles** in it. Trace the triangles.

Shapes

This picture has **triangles** in it. Trace the triangles.

Shapes

Color the **triangles**.

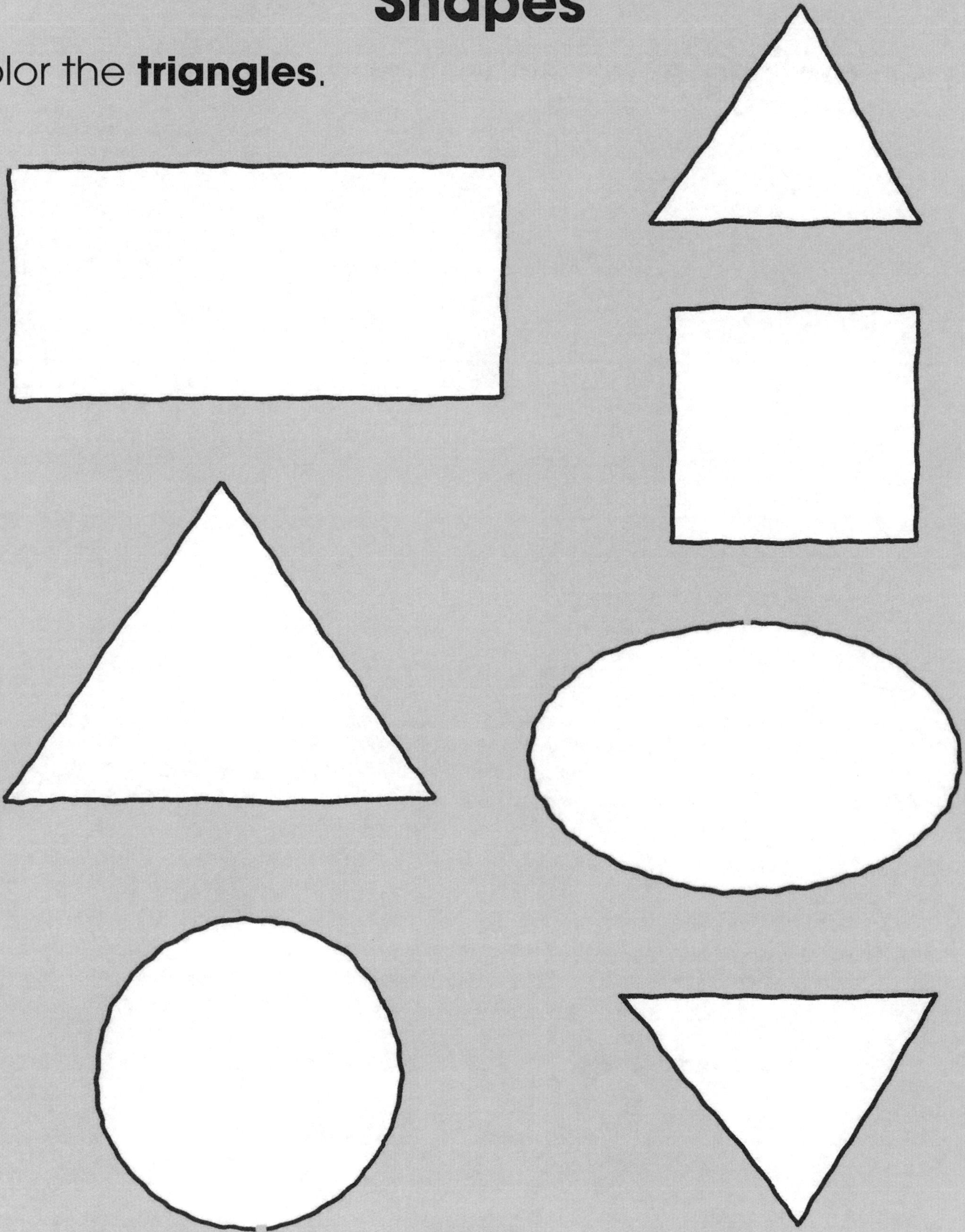

Shapes

This is a **rectangle**. Trace the shape.

Trace the word.

rectangle

Shapes

This picture has **rectangles** in it. Trace the rectangles.

Shapes

This picture has **rectangles** in it. Trace the rectangles.

Shapes

Color the **rectangles**.

Shapes

This is an **oval**. Trace the shape.

Trace the word.

oval

Shapes

This picture has **ovals** in it. Trace the ovals.

 Name ____________________

Shapes

This picture has **ovals** in it. Trace the ovals.

Shapes

Color the **ovals**.

Shapes

This is a **rhombus**. Trace the shape.

Trace the word.

rhombus

Shapes

This picture has **rhombuses** in it. Trace the rhombuses.

 Name ______________________

Shapes

This picture has **rhombuses** in it. Trace the rhombuses.

Shapes

Color the **rhombuses**.

Shapes

Draw a line to match each shape on the left to the same shape on the right.

Shapes

Draw a line to match each shape on the left to the same shape on the right.

 Name ____________________

Shapes

Draw a line to match each shape on the left to a picture with the same shape on the right.

Shapes

Draw a line to match each shape on the left to a picture with the same shape on the right.

Same Size

Circle the shape in each row that is the **same size** as the first shape.

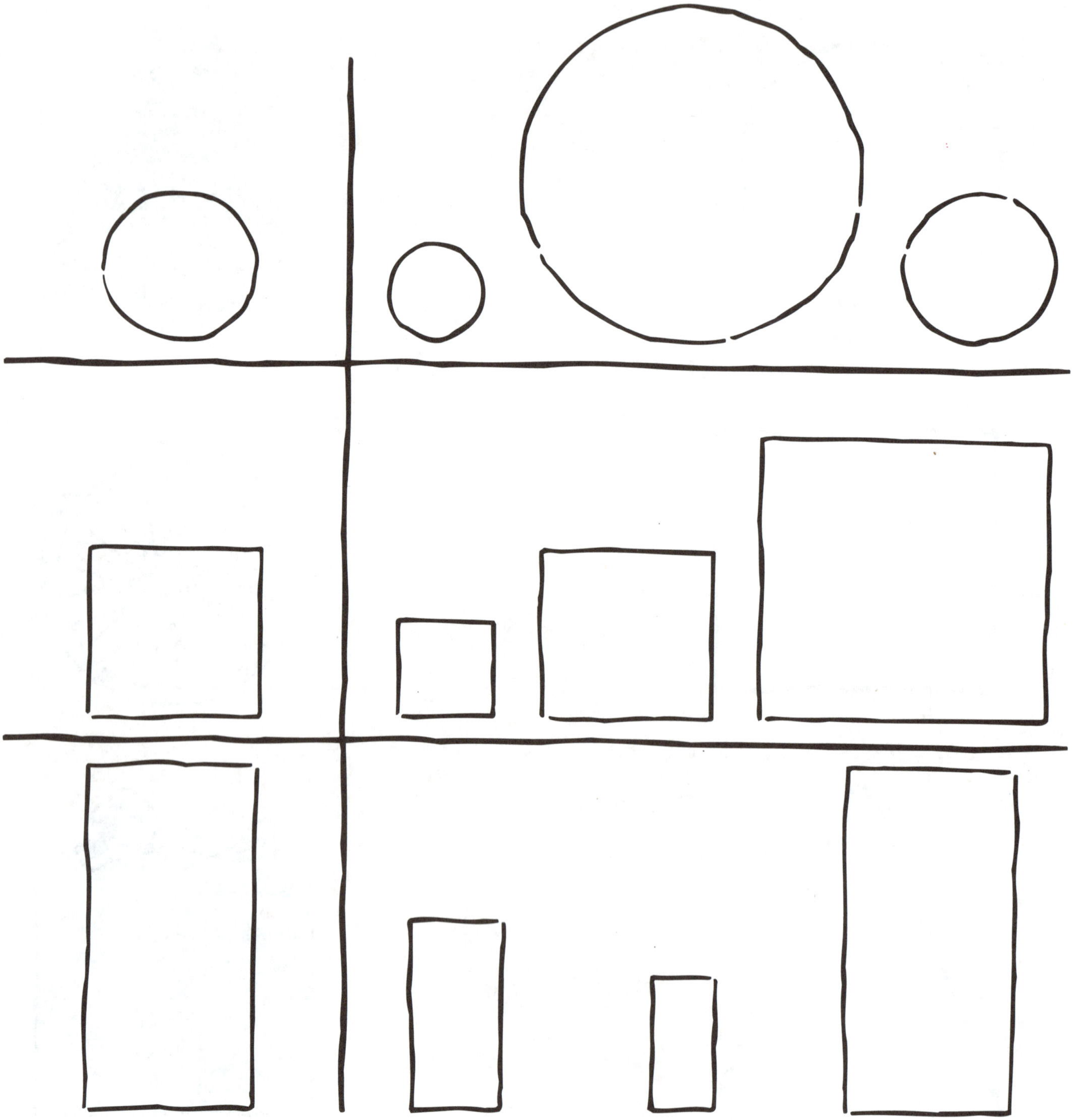

Same Size

Circle the shape in each row that is the **same size** as the first shape.

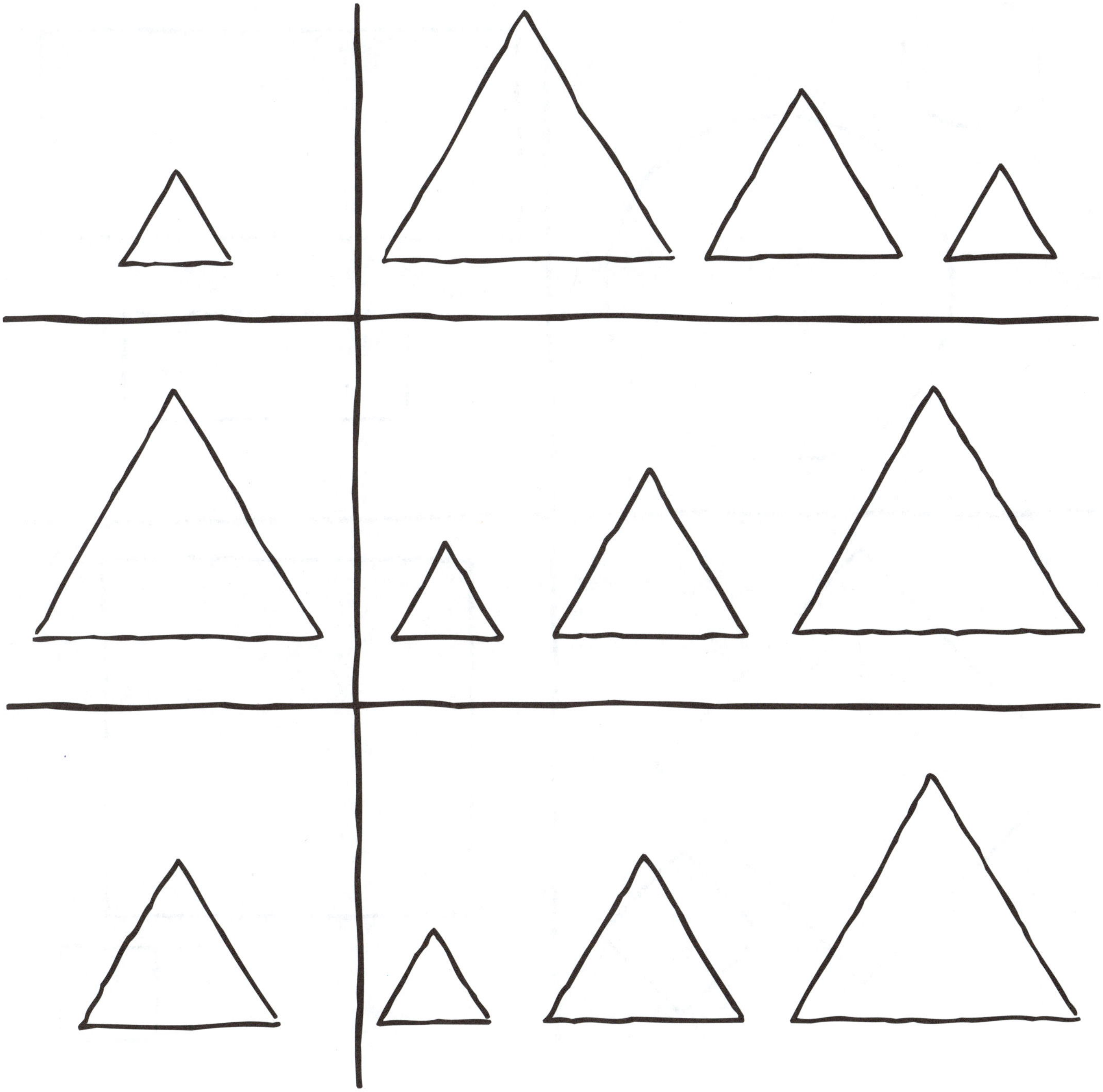

Big and Small

Color the **big** shape in each box. Draw a line under the **small** shape in each box.

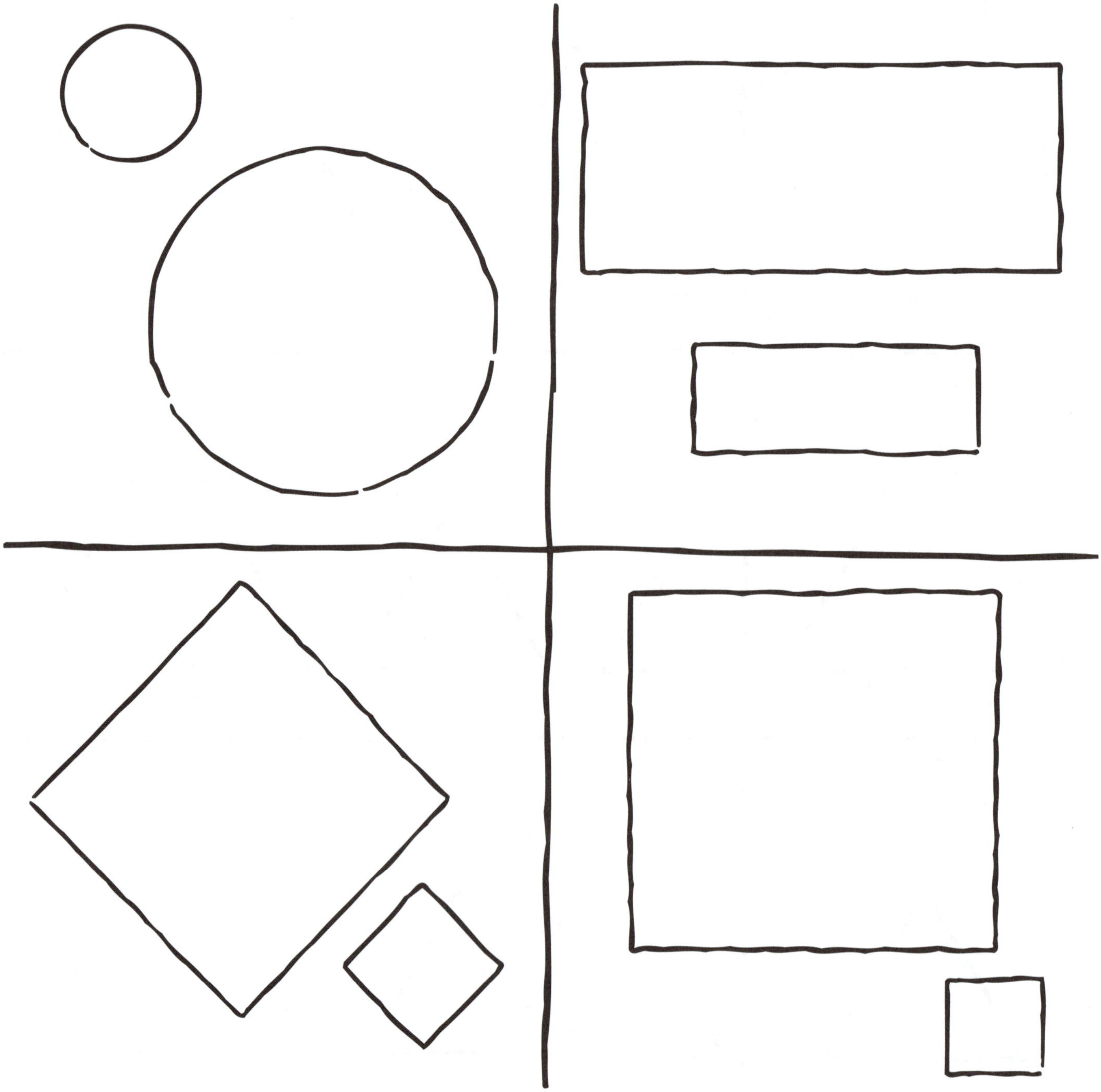

Big and Small

Draw a line to match the shapes that are the same. Then, color each **big** shape red and each **small** shape green.

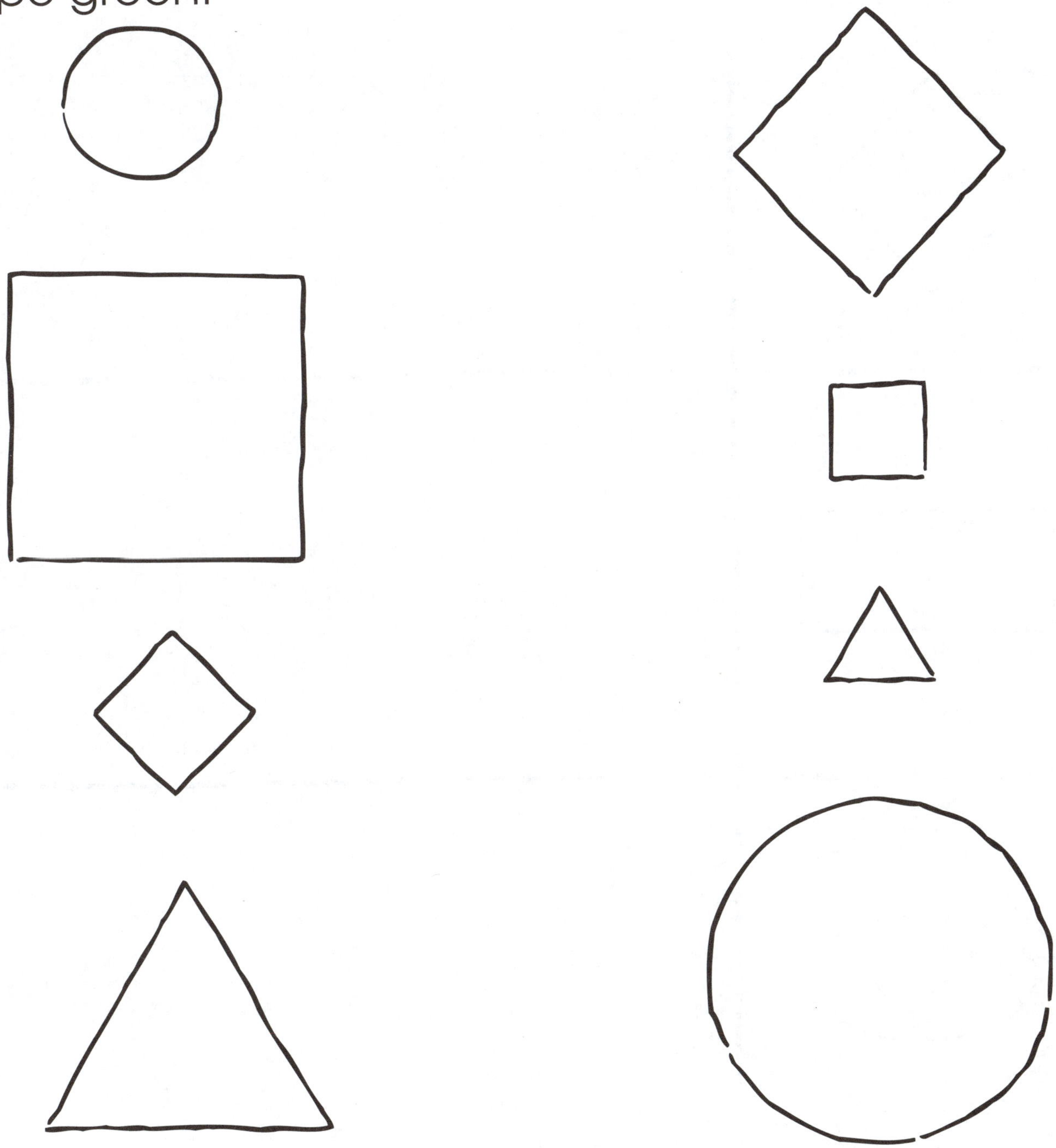

 Name ____________________

Bigger

Name the shape in the box. Then, draw the same shape again. Make your shape **bigger** than the one in the box.

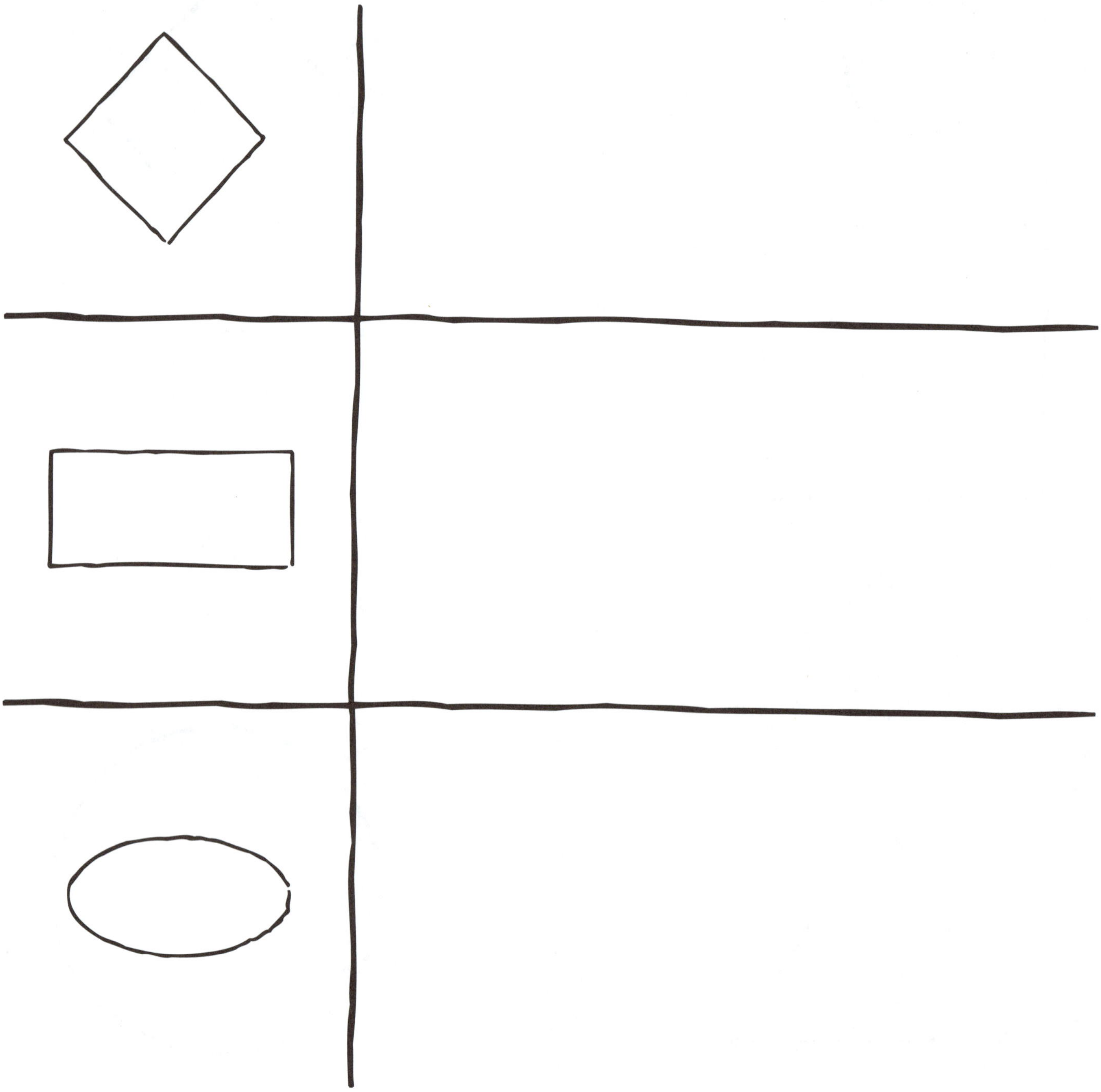

Smaller

Name the shape in the box. Then, draw the same shape again. Make your shape **smaller** than the one in the box.

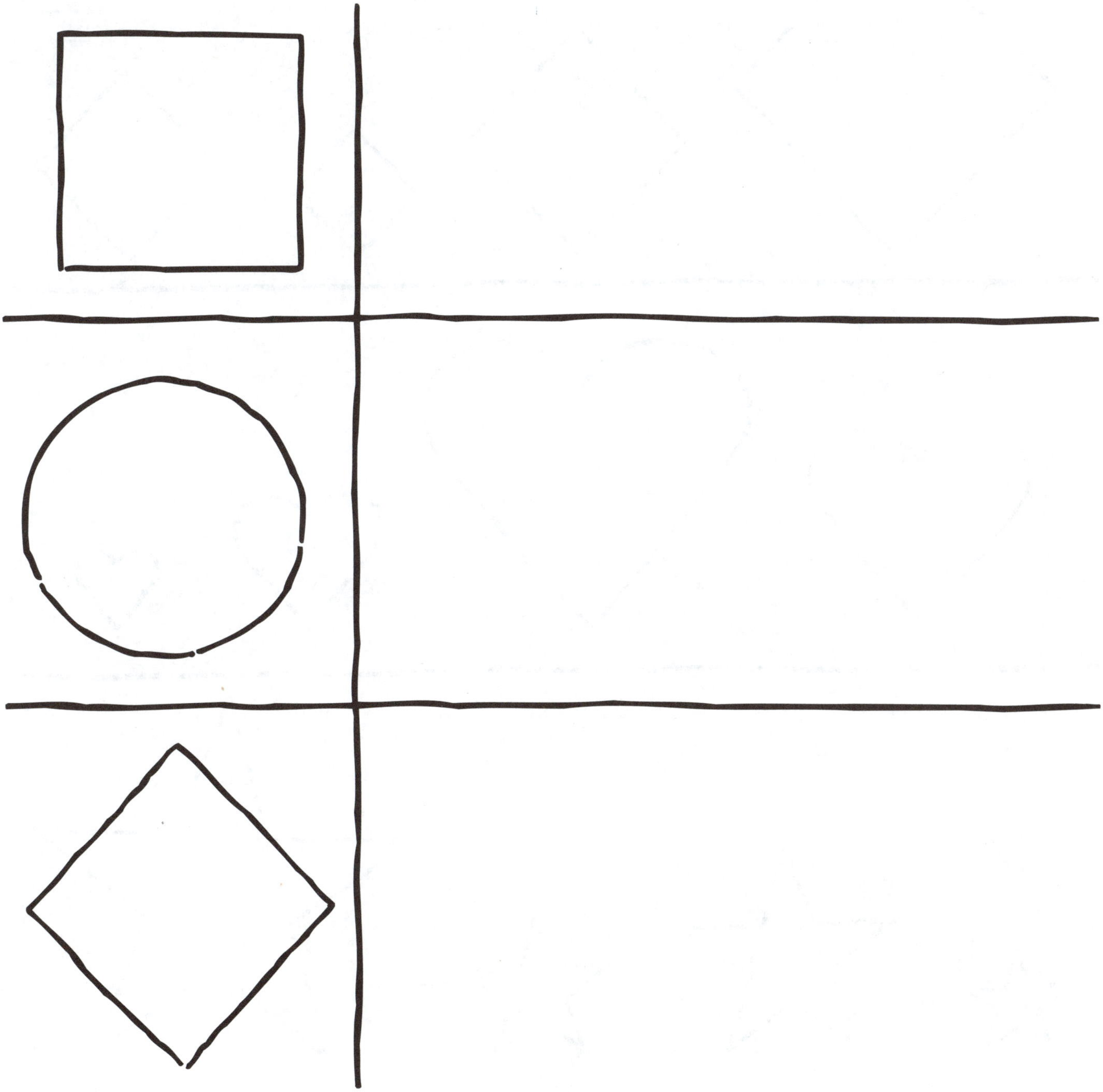

Biggest

Find the **biggest** shape in each row. Color it orange.

Smallest

Find the **smallest** shape in each row. Color it purple.

 Name ____________________

Short and Tall

Circle each **short** person below. Draw a line under each **tall** person.

Short and Tall

Draw a line to match the flowers that are the same. Then, color each **short** flower pink. Color each **tall** flower orange.

Shorter

Look at the glass below. Draw another glass beside it. Make your glass **shorter** than the first one.

Taller

Look at the table below. Draw another table beside it. Make your table **taller** than the first one.

 Name ____________________

Shortest

Circle the **shortest** candle in each row.

Tallest

Circle the **tallest** tree in each row.

 Name ______________________

Long and Short

Draw a line to match the pictures that are the same. Then, circle the **long** things. Draw a box around the **short** things.

Long and Short

Circle each **long** thing. Then, draw a line under each **short** thing.

Longer

Look at the girl's kite. Draw another kite beside it. Make the tail on your kite **longer** than the first one.

Shorter

Look at the top wagon. Draw a **shorter** handle on the bottom wagon.

Longest

Name the animals in each row. Then, circle the animal with the **longest** tail.

Shortest

Name the animals in each row. Then, circle the animal with the **shortest** tail.

Size Review

Color the **longest** crayon red. Color the **shortest** crayon purple.

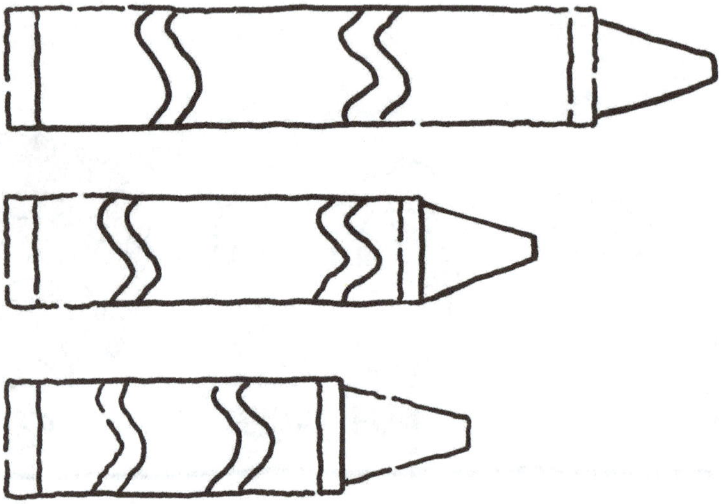

Circle the two bears that are the **same size**.

Size Review

Color the **biggest** ball blue. Color the **smallest** ball green.

Draw a line under the **shortest** tree. Circle the **tallest** tree.

Opposites

Look at the picture. Trace the word.

big

Opposites

Look at the picture. Trace the word.

little

 Name ______________________

Opposites

Look at the picture. Trace the word.

slow

Opposites

Look at the picture. Trace the word.

fast

Name ______________________

Opposites

Look at the picture. Trace the word.

in

Opposites

Look at the picture. Trace the word.

out

Opposites

Look at the picture. Trace the word.

top

Opposites

Look at the picture. Trace the word.

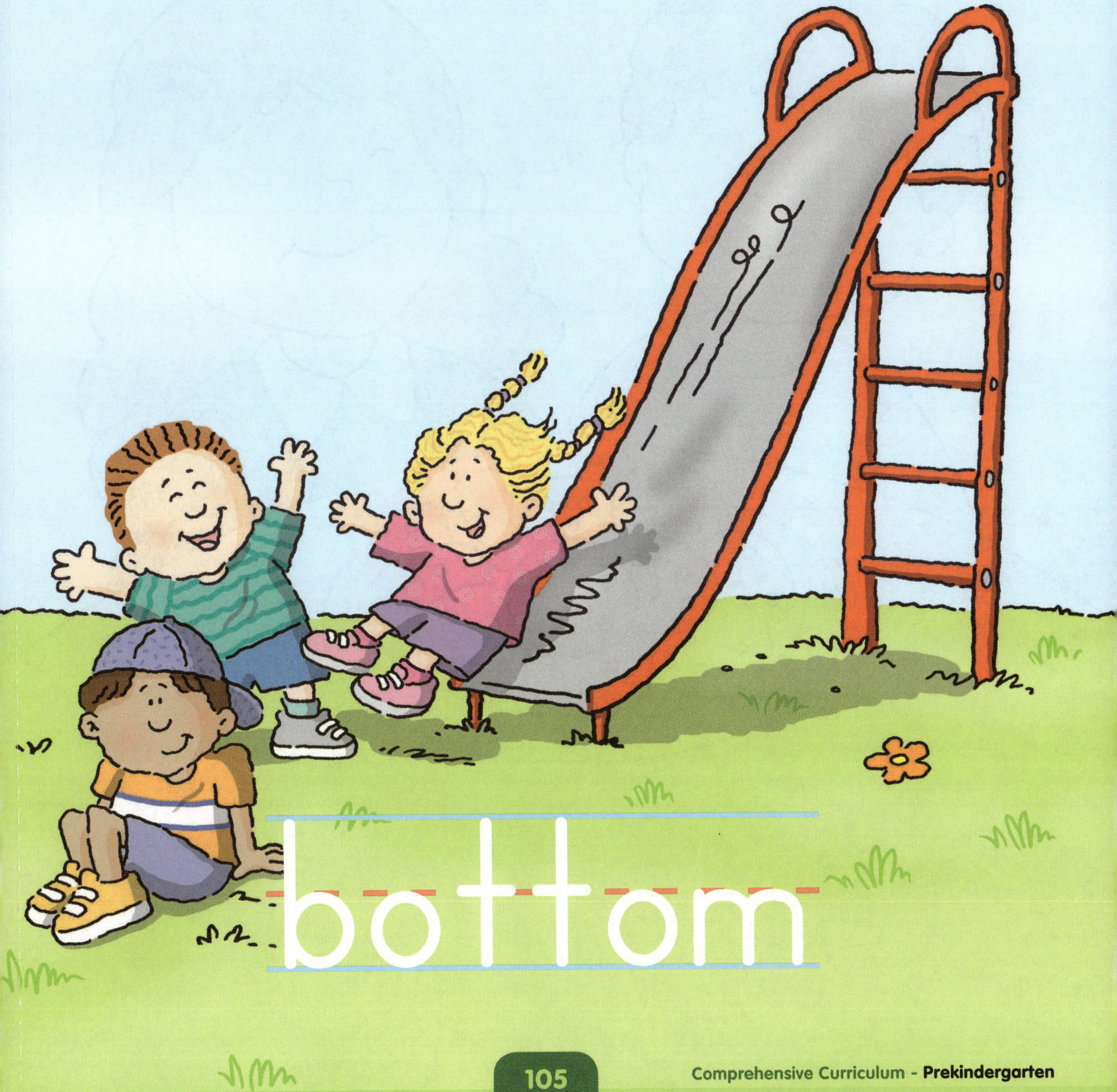

bottom

Opposites

Look at the picture. Trace the word.

full

Opposites

Look at the picture. Trace the word.

empty

 Name ____________________

Opposites

Look at the picture. Trace the word.

happy

Opposites

Look at the picture. Trace the word.

sad

 Name ____________________

Opposites

Look at the picture. Trace the word.

up

Opposites

Look at the picture. Trace the word.

down

 Name ____________________

Opposites

Look at the picture. Trace the word.

over

Opposites

Look at the picture. Trace the word.

under

Opposites

Look at the picture. Trace the word.

old

Opposites

Look at the picture. Trace the word.

new

Opposites

Look at the picture. Trace the word.

wet

Opposites

Look at the picture. Trace the word.

dry

 Name ________________

Opposites

Look at the picture. Trace the word.

Opposites

Look at the picture. Trace the word.

cold

Opposites

Look at the picture. Trace the word.

left

Opposites

Look at the picture. Trace the word.

right

Opposites

Look at the picture. Trace the word.

front

Opposites

Look at the picture. Trace the word.

back

Opposites

Look at the picture. Trace the word.

above

Opposites

Look at the picture. Trace the word.

below

Opposites

Draw a line to match each picture with its opposite.

full

out

in

short

tall

empty

Opposites

Draw a line to match each picture with its opposite.

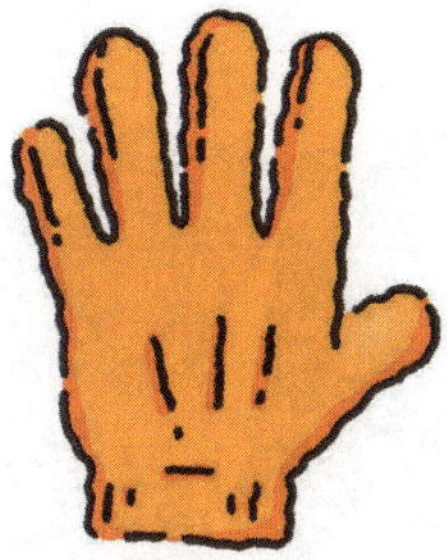

left

sad

above

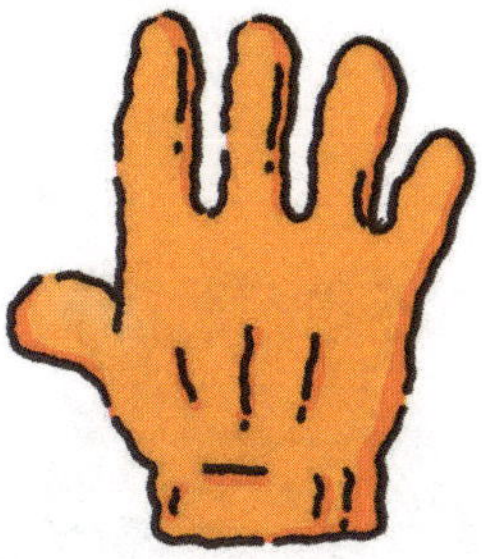

right

happy

below

Opposites

Draw a line to match each picture with its opposite.

big

out

front

little

in

back

Opposites

Look at the pictures in each row. Circle the picture that is the opposite of the first picture in each row.

Opposites

Look at the pictures in each row. Circle the picture that is the opposite of the first picture in each row.

Opposites

Cut out the pictures at the bottom of the page. Glue them in the correct places.

- Put the brown bear **inside** the house.
- Put the gray bear **outside** the house.
- Put the red bird **up** in the tree.
- Put the yellow bird **down** on the ground.

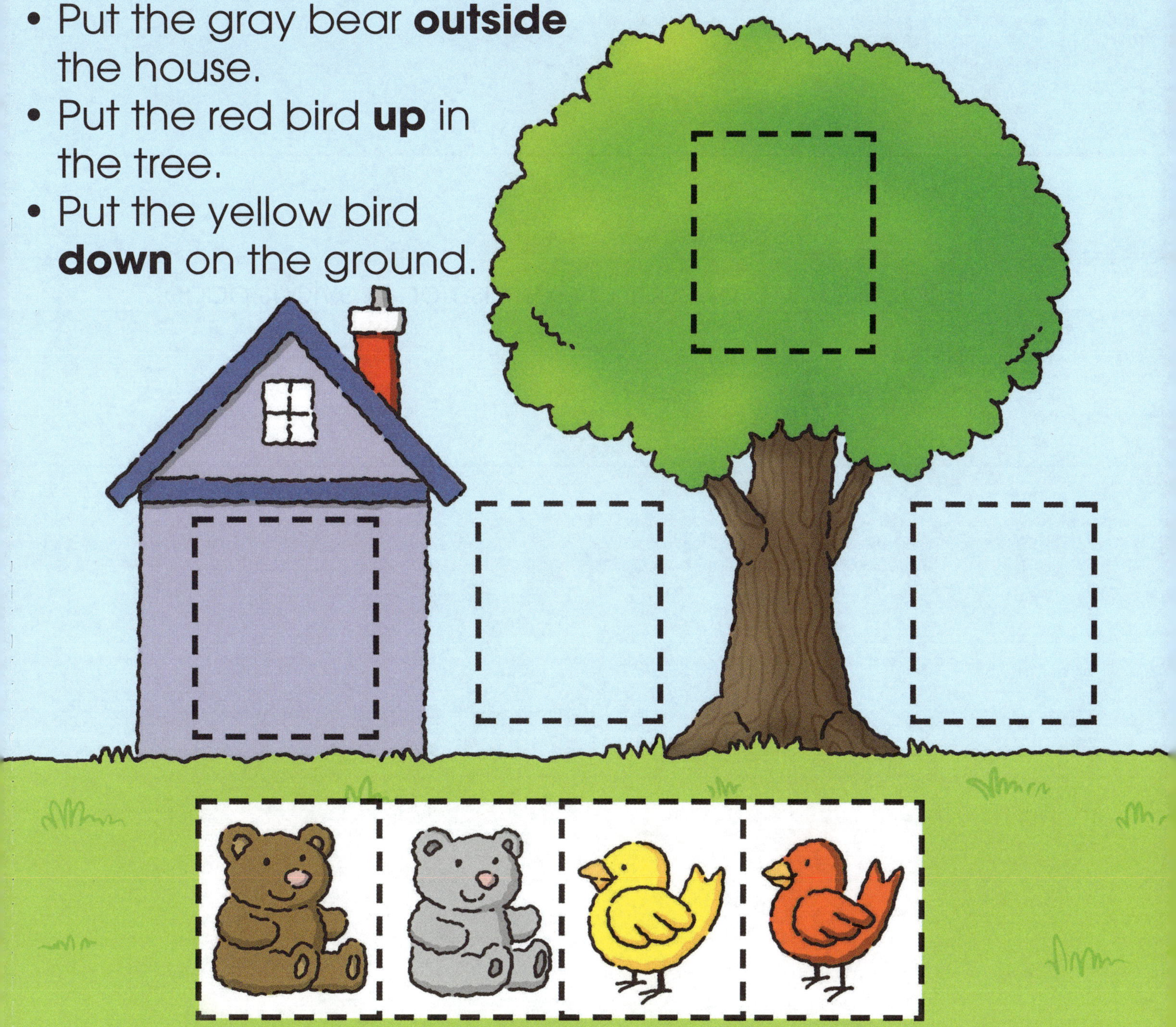

Page is blank for cutting exercise on previous page.

Opposite Puzzles

Cut out the puzzle pieces below and on pages 135 and 137. Mix them up. Then, put the matching puzzle pieces together.

big

hot

little

cold

Page is blank for cutting exercise on previous page.

Opposite Puzzles

hard

up

soft

down

Page is blank for cutting exercise on previous page.

Opposite Puzzles

wet

short

dry

long

Page is blank for cutting exercise on previous page.

Go-Togethers

Look at the pictures in each row. Circle the picture that goes together with the first picture.

 Name ____________________

Go-Togethers

Look at the pictures in each row. Circle the picture that goes together with the first picture.

Go-Togethers

Look at the pictures in each row. Cross out the picture that does not belong with the others.

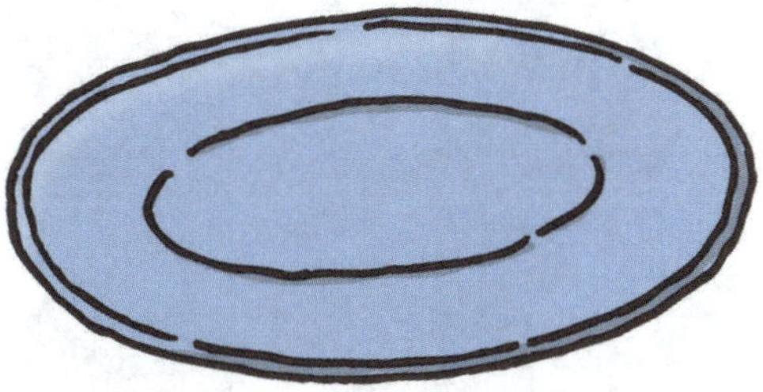

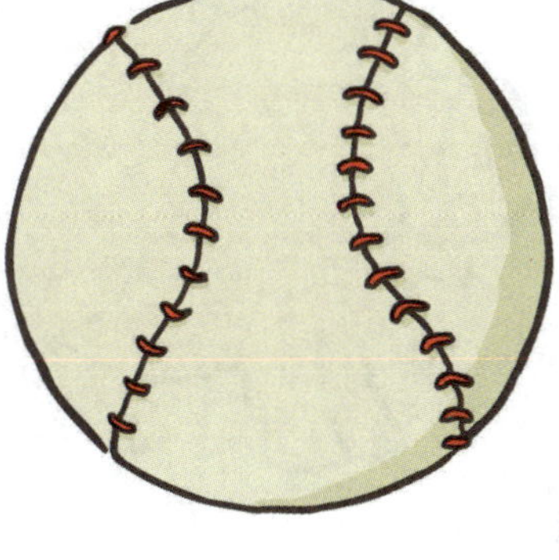
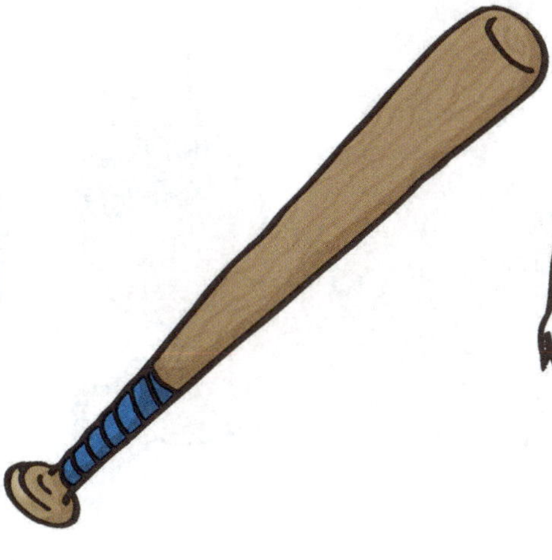

Go-Togethers

Look at the pictures in each row. Cross out the picture that does not belong with the others.

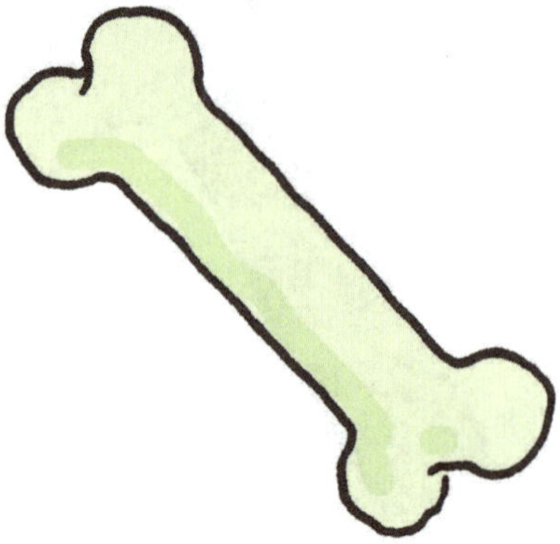

Same

Look at the pictures in each row. Circle the picture that is the **same** as the first picture in each row.

Same

Look at the pictures in each row. Circle the picture that is the **same** as the first picture in each row.

Different

Look at the pictures in each row. Circle the picture that is **different** in each row.

Different

Look at the pictures in each row. Circle the picture that is **different** in each row.

Animal Matching

Play a matching game with animals.

1. Cut out the pictures below. Put them in a paper bag. Then, shake the bag.
2. Pull out two pictures. If they are the same, keep them.
3. If the pictures are different, put them back in the bag and try again.
4. When you have matched all the cards, the game is over.

Page is blank for cutting exercise on previous page.

Same

Look at the shapes in each row. Color the shape that is the **same** as the first shape in each row.

Same

Look at the shapes in each row. Color the shape that is the **same** as the first shape in each row.

Different

Color the shape in each row that is **different**.

Name ______________________

Different

Color the shape in each row that is **different**.

Same

Look at the letters in each row. Circle the letter that is the **same** as the first letter in each row.

E	F	E
R	B	R
M	M	N

Same

Look at the letters in each row. Circle the letter that is the **same** as the first letter in each row.

O	O	C
T	T	I
J	L	J

Same

Look at the letters in each row. Circle the letter that is the **same** as the first letter in each row.

u	u	n
d	b	d
h	h	n

Same

Look at the letters in each row. Circle the letter that is the **same** as the first letter in each row.

v	v	y
l	i	l
f	t	f

Letter Matching

Play a matching game with letter cookies.

1. Cut out the letter cookies below.
2. Mix up the cards. Then, put them letter-side down on a table.
3. Turn over two cards at a time. If the letters are the same, keep them.
4. If the letters are different, put them back on the table.
5. Play until no cards are left.

Page is blank for cutting exercise on previous page.

Same

In each row, circle all the words that are the **same** as the first one.

put	put	pat	put
bed	bet	bed	bed
man	man	men	can

Same

In each row, circle all the words that are the **same** as the first one.

cat	cat	sat	cat
pot	pat	pot	pot
fin	fin	fin	fin

Same

In each row, circle the word that is the **same** as the first one.

jam	ham	jam
pot	pot	got
set	met	set

Same

In each row, circle the word that is the **same** as the first one.

mug	mug	bug
bat	mat	bat
pin	tin	pin

WRITING READINESS

Name ______________________________

Left to Right

Help the cat get to the milk. Follow the arrow to trace a path to the milk.

Help the rabbit get to the carrot. Follow the arrow to trace a path to the carrot.

Left to Right

Help the bear get to the honey. Follow the arrow to trace a path to the honey.

Help the cow get to the grass. Follow the arrow to trace a path to the grass.

Name ______________________

Left to Right

Trace the lines from **left** to **right** to help each mother find her baby.

Left to Right

Trace the lines from **left** to **right** to help each mother find her baby.

Name ____________________

Left to Right

Trace the lines from **left** to **right** to help each mother find her baby.

Left to Right

Trace the lines from **left** to **right** to help each animal get home.

Name ______________________

Left to Right

Trace the lines from **left** to **right** to help each animal get home.

Left to Right

Trace the lines from **left** to **right** to help each animal find something it likes to eat.

Name ____________________

Left to Right

Trace the lines from **left** to **right** to help each animal find something it likes to eat.

Top to Bottom

Trace the lines from **top** to **bottom** to make each caterpillar's legs.

Name ____________________

Top to Bottom

Help the children hold on to their balloons. Trace the balloon strings from **top** to **bottom**.

Top to Bottom

Help the spiders make their web. Trace the lines from **top** to **bottom**.

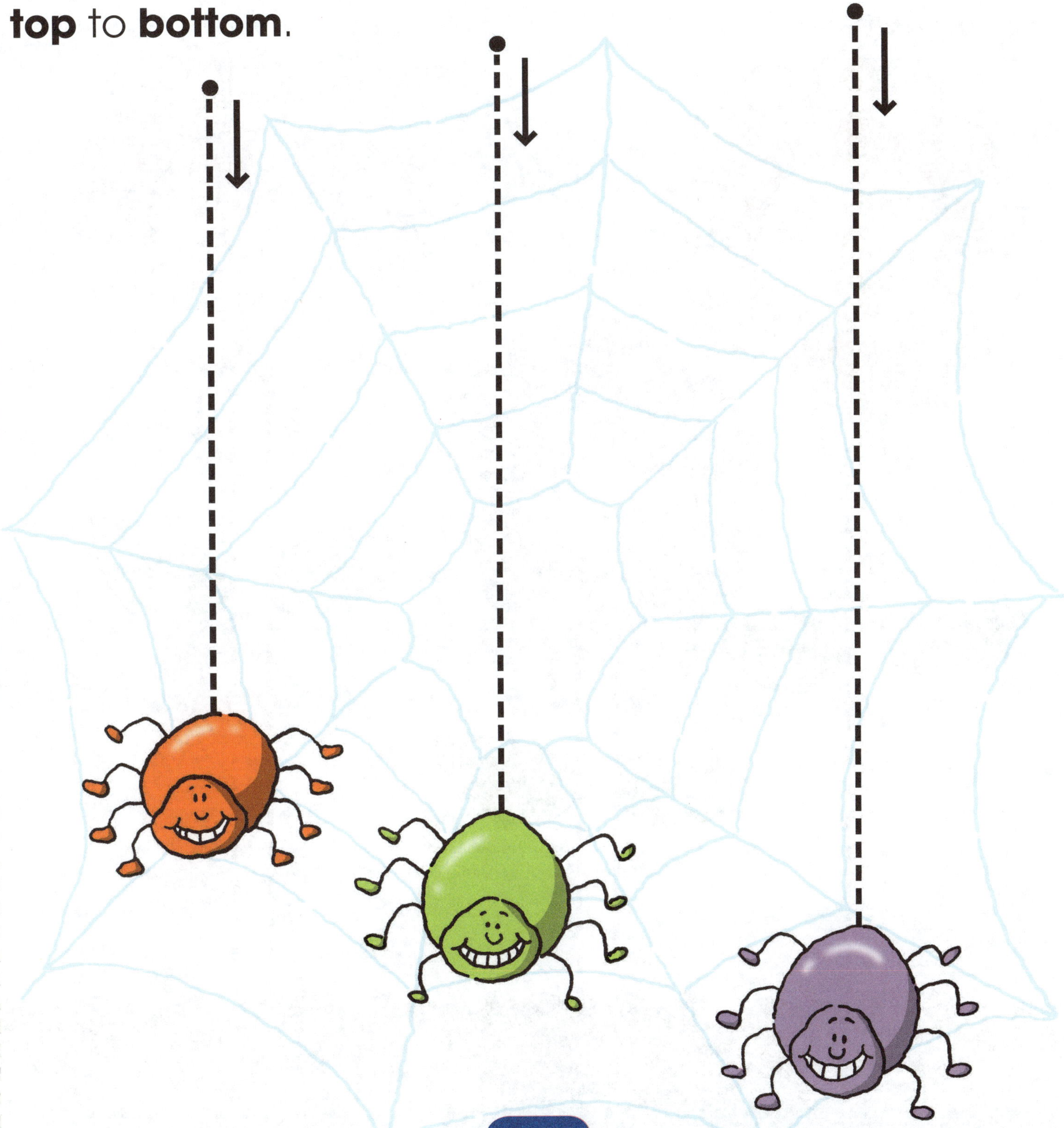

Name ____________________

Top to Bottom

Trace the lines from **top** to **bottom** to make stems on the flowers.

Top to Bottom

Help the girl paint the fence. Trace the lines from **top** to **bottom**.

 Name ____________________

Slanted Lines

Help the children slide down the hill. Trace the lines from **top** to **bottom**.

Slanted Lines

Help the children go down the slides. Trace the lines from **top** to **bottom**.

 Name ____________________

Curved Lines

Trace each ball's bounces from **left** to **right**.

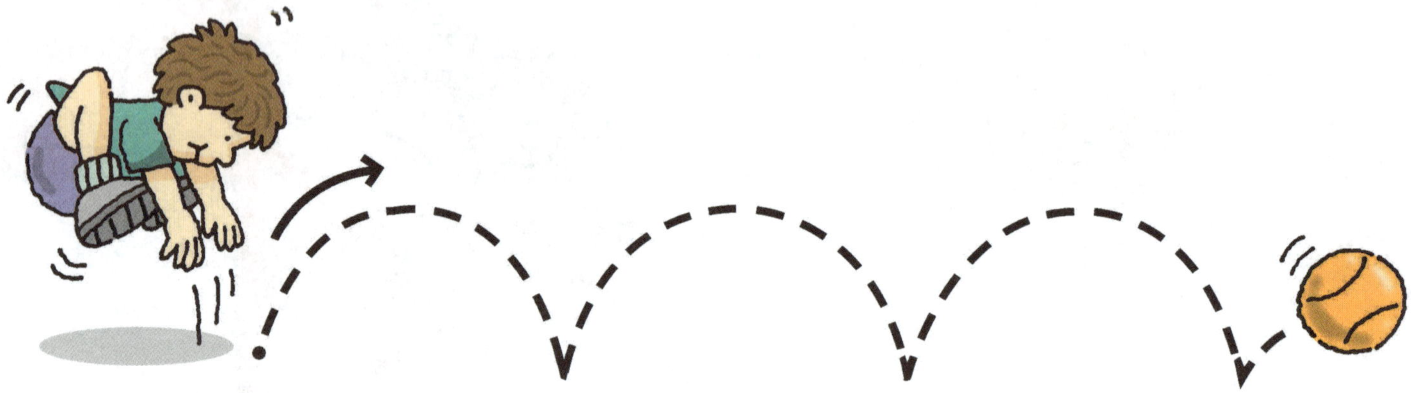

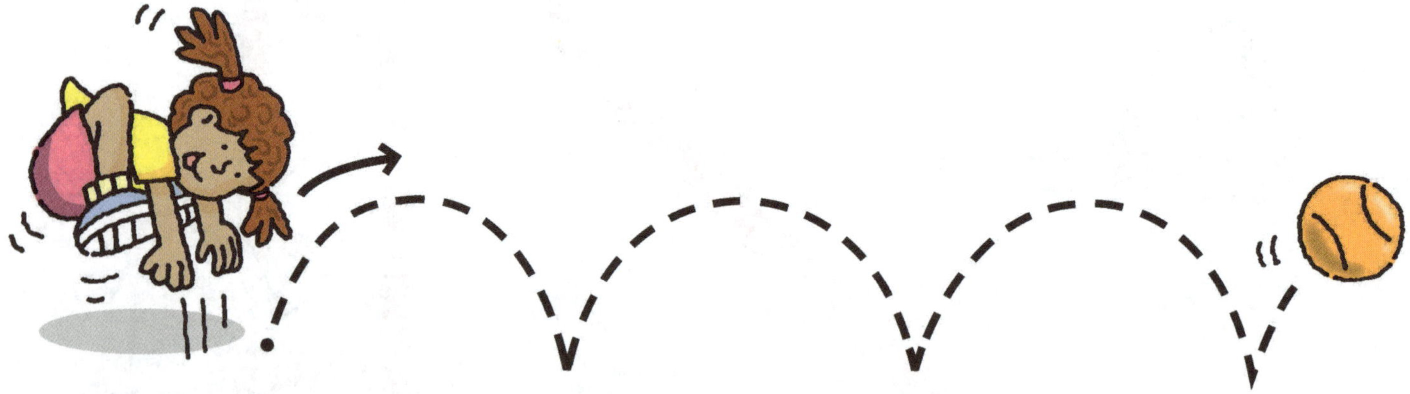

Now, draw this ball's bounces on your own.

Curved Lines

Trace each bee's path from **left** to **right**.

Now, draw this bee's path on your own.

Name ______________________

Curved Lines

Trace each kangaroo's jumps from **left** to **right**.

Now, draw this kangaroo's jumps on your own.

Curved Lines

Trace each ocean wave from **left** to **right**. Then, draw an ocean wave of your own.

Name ______________________

Forward Circles

Follow the arrows to trace the circles on each scoop of ice cream.

Forward Circles

Follow the arrows to trace each circle on the sun and the flowers.

Name ____________________

Backward Circles

Follow the arrows to trace the plates on the picnic table.

Backward Circles

Follow the arrows to trace each circle on the lollipops.

Name ______________________

Top-to-Bottom Lines

Start at the top. Follow the arrows to trace the dotted lines.

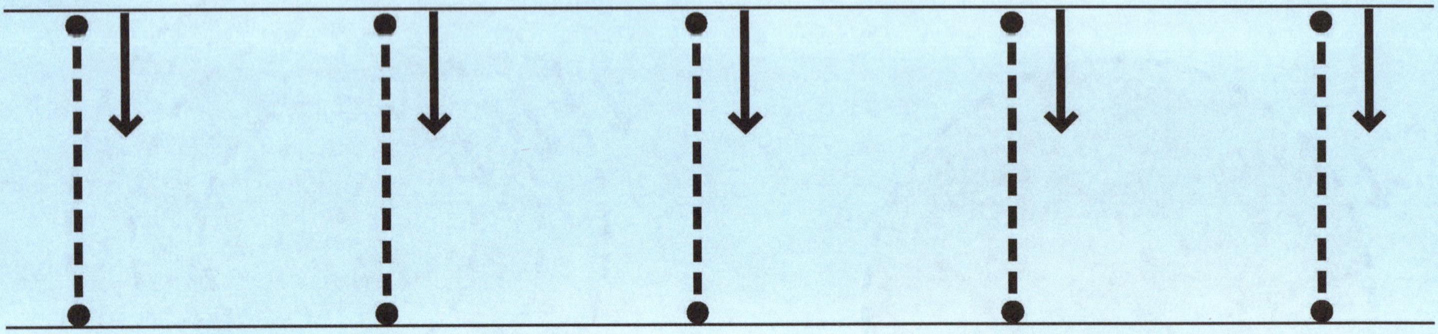

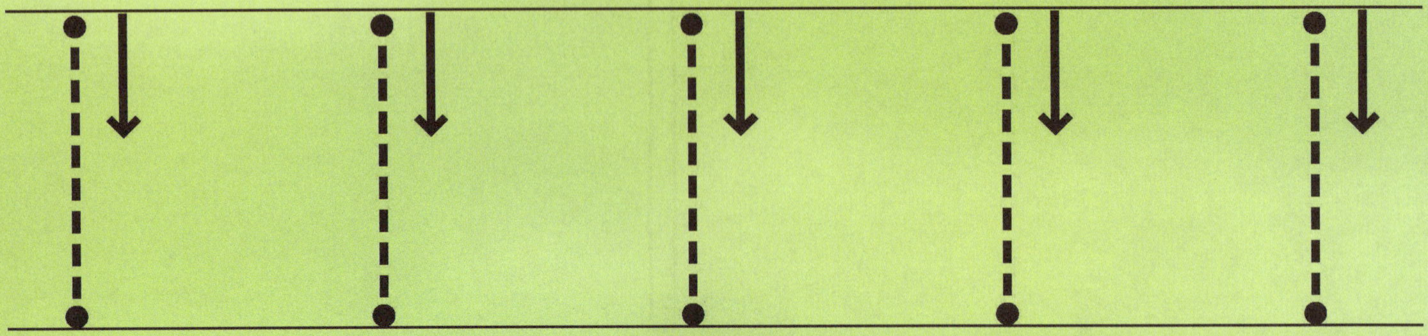

Slanted Lines

Start at the top. Follow the arrows to trace the dotted lines.

Name ____________________

Slanted Lines

Start at the top. Follow the arrows to trace the dotted lines.

Curved Lines

Start at the dots on the left. Follow the arrows to trace the dotted lines.

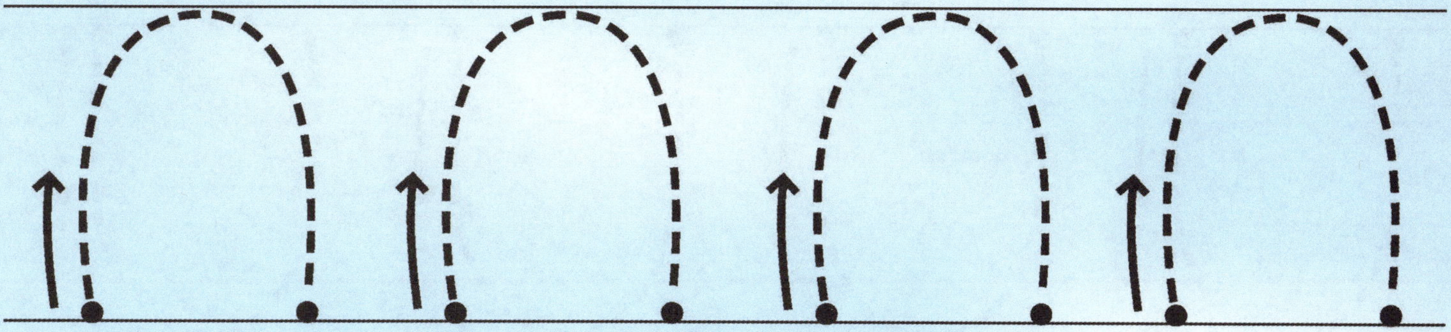

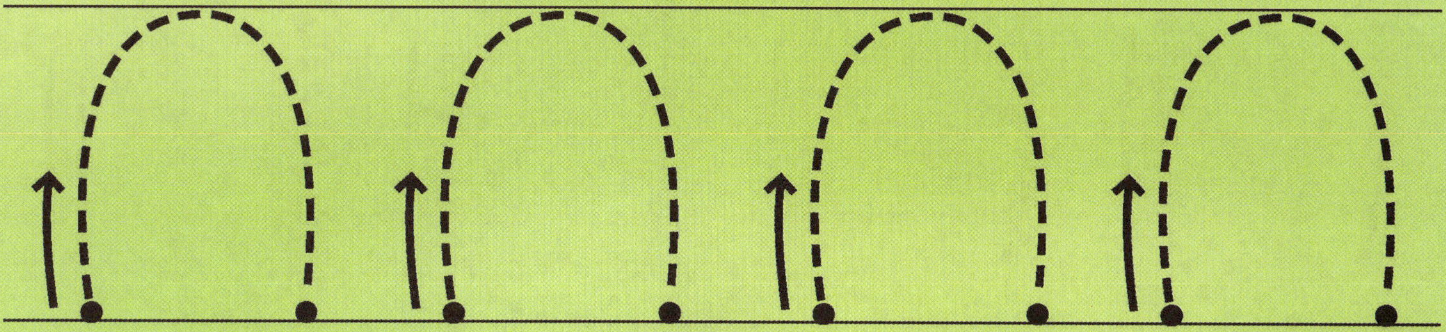

Name ______________________

Curved Lines

Start at the dots on the right. Follow the arrows to trace the dotted lines.

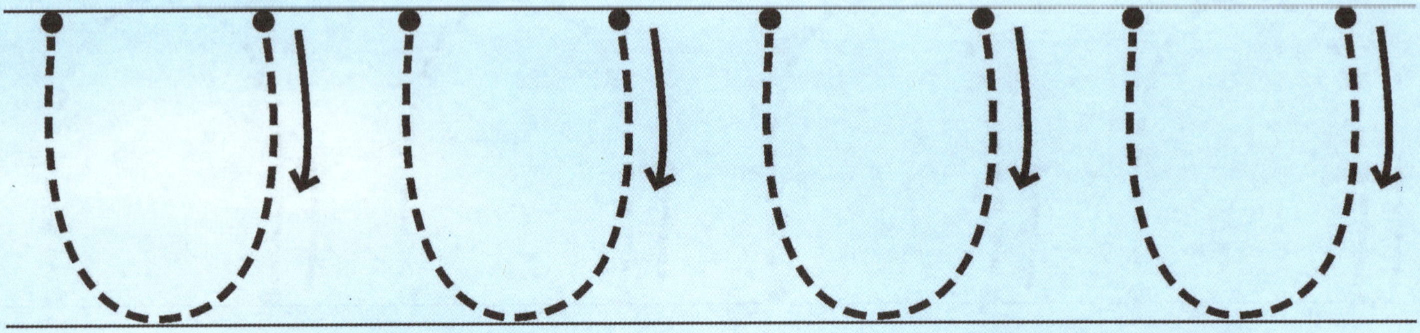

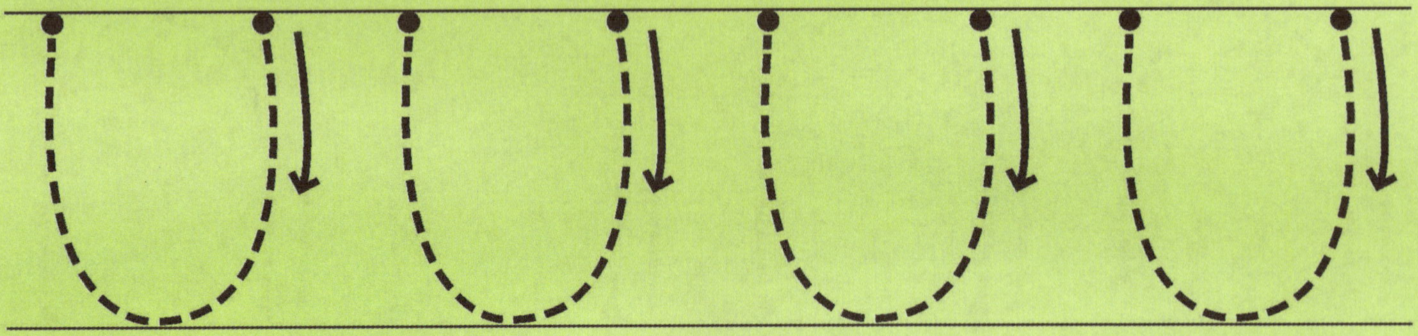

Ovals

Start at the dots. Follow the arrows to trace the dotted lines.

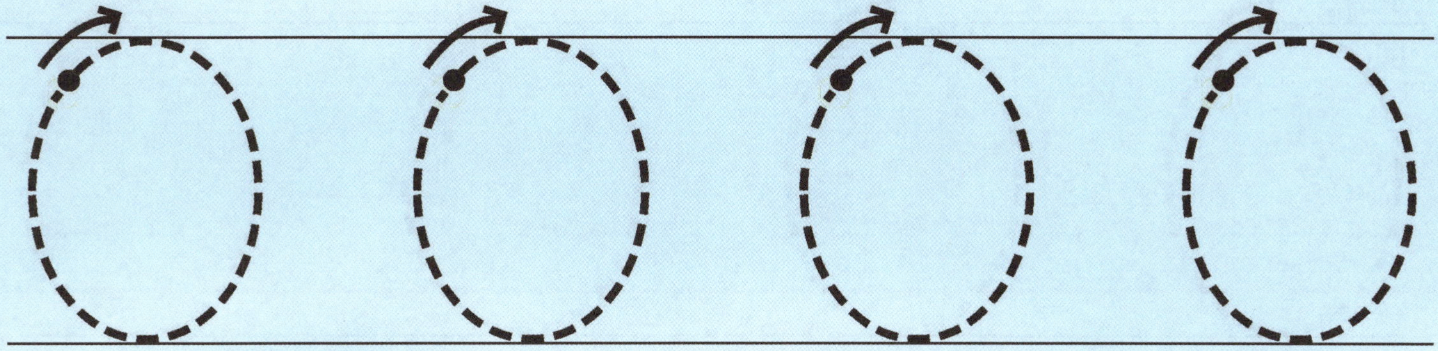

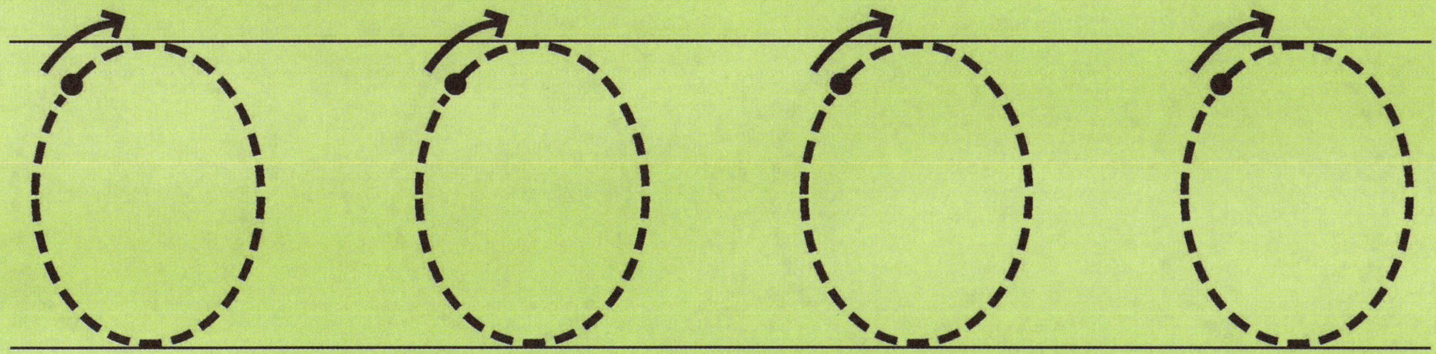

Name ____________________

Ovals

Start at the dots. Follow the arrows to trace the dotted lines.

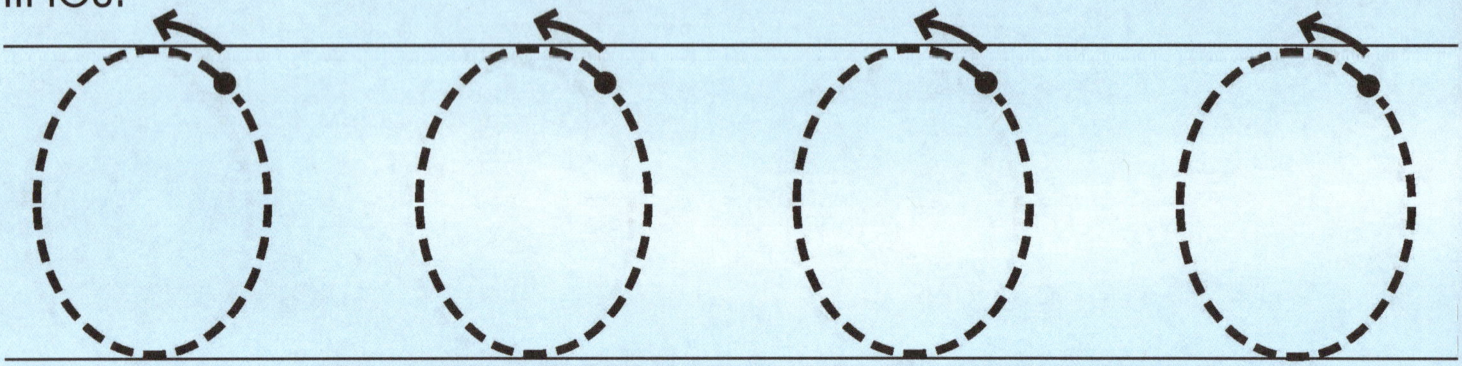

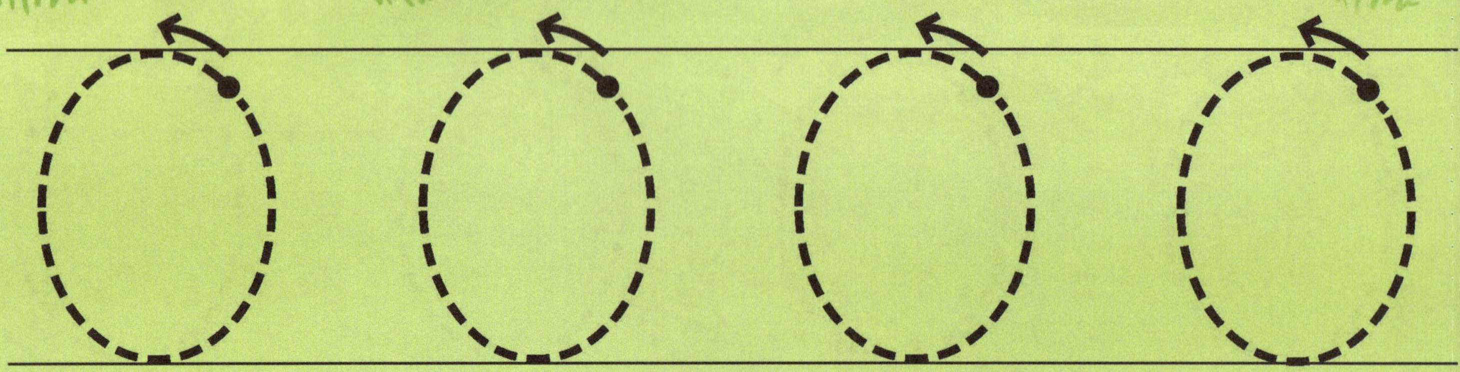

READING READINESS

Name ______________________

Trace UPPERCASE **A**.

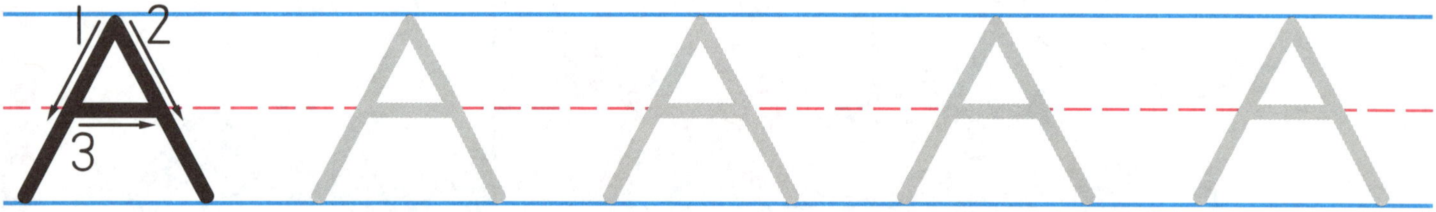

Now, write UPPERCASE **A**.

Trace lowercase **a**.

Now, write lowercase **a**.

Name ____________________

Letter Aa

Say the names of the pictures. Color each picture that begins with the sound of **Aa**.

Letter Aa

Say the names of the pictures on the apples. Cut out each apple that has a picture that begins with the sound of **Aa**. Glue the **Aa** apples in the bowl.

Page is blank for cutting exercise on previous page.

Letter Aa

Color the **A**'s **red**. Color the **a**'s **green**. Color the other letters **yellow**.

Name ____________________

Trace UPPERCASE **B**.

Now, write UPPERCASE **B**.

Trace lowercase **b**.

b b b b b b b

Now, write lowercase **b**.

Name ______________________

Letter Bb

Draw a line from each letter **b** to a picture that begins with that sound.

b

b

b

Name ____________________

Letter Bb

Help the bear get to the honey. Use a crayon to trace the **Bb** path to the honey tree.

Name ______________________

Trace UPPERCASE **C**.

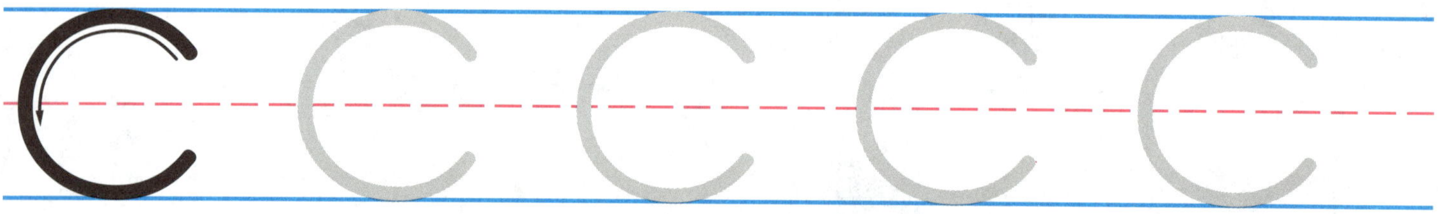

Now, write UPPERCASE **C**.

Trace lowercase **c**.

c c c c c c c

Now, write lowercase **c**.

Name ______________________

Letter Cc

Say the names of the pictures. Color each picture that begins with the sound of **Cc**.

Letter Cc

Match the cups and saucers. Cut out the cups with pictures that begin with the **Cc** sound. Then, glue them on the **Cc** saucers.

Page is blank for cutting exercise on previous page.

Letter Cc

Look at the patterns on the cats' sweaters. Draw a line between the cats with matching **Cc** patterns on their sweaters.

Name ____________________

Letter Review

Look at the letter each person is holding. Circle the same letter in each box.

Letter Review

Look at the letter each person is holding. Circle the same letter in each box.

g b k

o a c

Name ____________________

Trace UPPERCASE **D**.

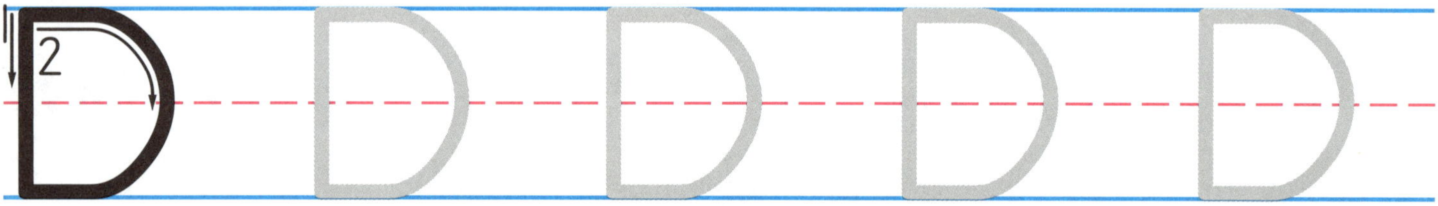

Now, write UPPERCASE **D**.

Trace lowercase **d**.

Now, write lowercase **d**.

Name ___________________________

Letter Dd

Say the names of the pictures. Color each picture that begins with the sound of **Dd**.

Letter Dd

Help the dolphin jump through the rings. Color the rings that have the letter **D** or **d** in them.

Name ____________________

Trace UPPERCASE **E**.

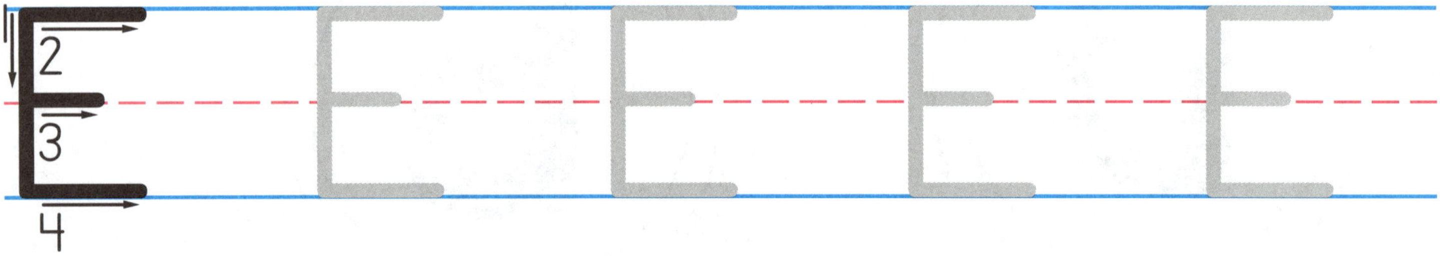

Now, write UPPERCASE **E**.

Trace lowercase **e**.

e e e e e e e

Now, write lowercase **e**.

Letter Ee

Say the names of the pictures. Color each picture that begins with the sound of **Ee**.

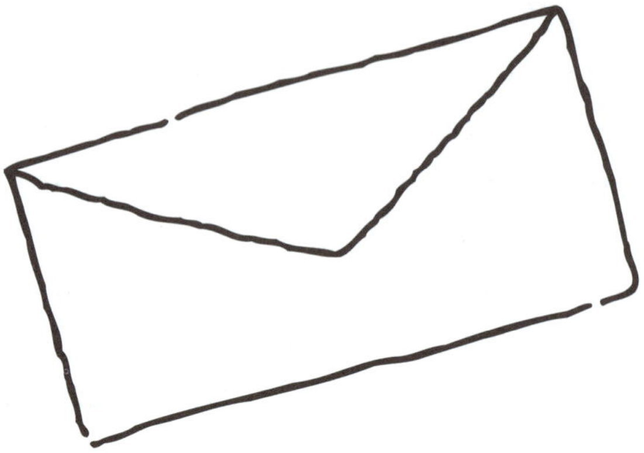

Letter Ee

Help the baby elephant get to its mother. Color the footprints with **E** or **e** on them.

 Name ____________________

Letter Ee

Trace the letter **E** or **e** on each egg.

Letter Review

Trace the letters on the caterpillar. Write the missing letters where they belong.

Name ______________________________

Trace UPPERCASE **F**.

Now, write UPPERCASE **F**.

Trace lowercase **f**.

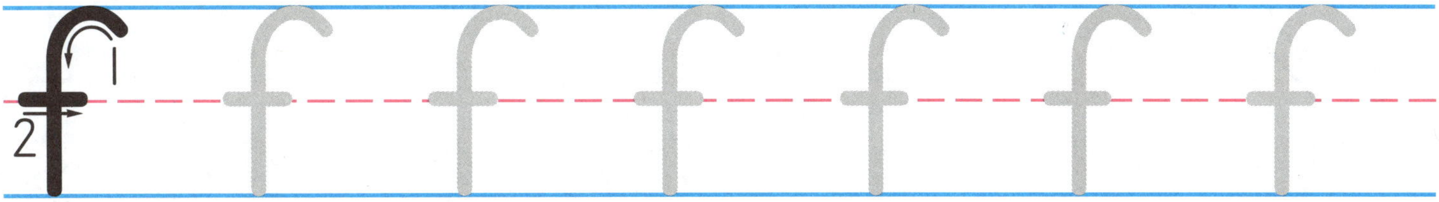

Now, write lowercase **f**.

Name ______________________________

Letter Ff

Say the names of the pictures. Color each picture that begins with the sound of **Ff**.

Letter Ff

Say the names of the pictures on the frogs. Cut out each frog that has a picture that begins with the sound of **Ff**. Then, glue the **Ff** frogs on the lily pads.

Page is blank for cutting exercise on previous page.

Letter Ff

Color the fish in the fish bowl.

- Color the **F** fish **orange**.
- Color the **f** fish **green**.
- Color the other fish with a color you like.

Name ______________________________

Trace UPPERCASE **G**.

Now, write UPPERCASE **G**.

Trace lowercase **g**.

g g g g g g g

Now, write lowercase **g**.

Name ______________________

Letter Gg

Say the names of the pictures. Color each picture that begins with the sound of **Gg**.

Letter Gg

Circle the letter **G** or **g** in each box.

Name ____________________

Letter Review

Draw a line from the UPPERCASE letter on each kite to the lowercase letter that matches.

d

b

p

t

f

e

Letter Review

Draw a line from the UPPERCASE letter on each kite to the lowercase letter that matches.

q

p

g

e

f

a

Name ____________________

Trace UPPERCASE **H**.

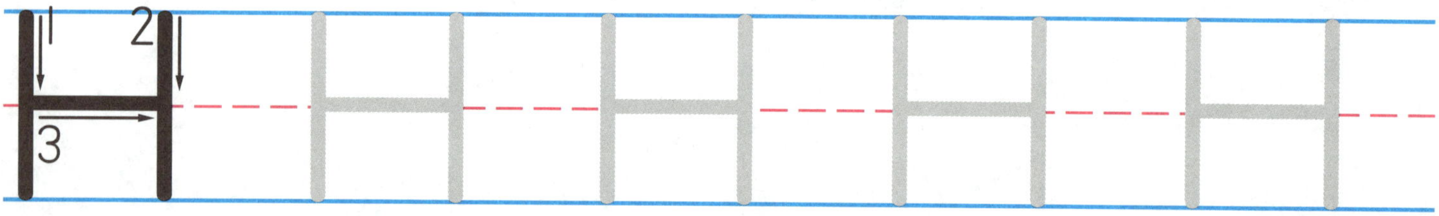

Now, write UPPERCASE **H**.

Trace lowercase **h**.

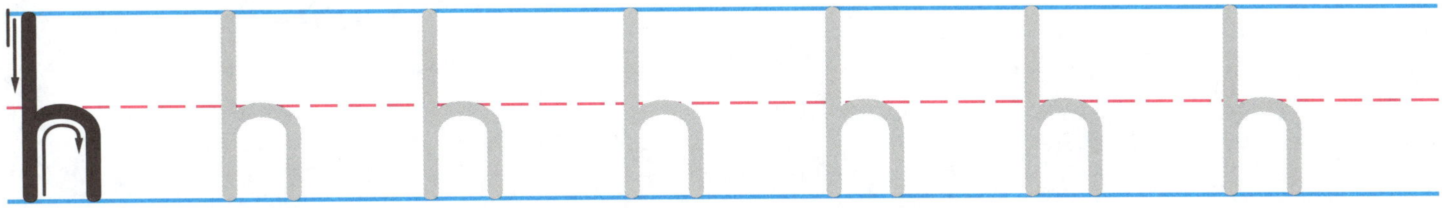

Now, write lowercase **h**.

Name ___________________________

Letter Hh

Say the names of the pictures. Color each picture that begins with the sound of **Hh**.

Letter Hh

Draw a line to match each hat to the person who wears it.

Name ______________________________

Trace UPPERCASE **I**.

Now, write UPPERCASE **I**.

Trace lowercase **i**.

Now, write lowercase **i**.

 Name ______________________

Letter Ii

Say the names of the pictures. Color each picture that begins with the sound of **Ii**.

Letter Ii

Help build the igloo. Trace the letters **I** and **i** below.

Name ____________________

Letter Ii

Help the inchworm get to the flower. Circle the letters **I** and **i**.

Letter Review

Trace the letters on the teddy bears. Write the missing letters where they belong.

 Name ______________________

Trace UPPERCASE **J**.

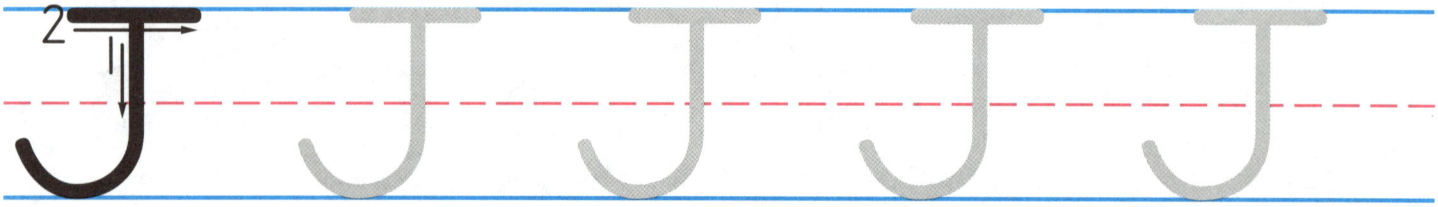

Now, write UPPERCASE **J**.

Trace lowercase **j**.

Now, write lowercase **j**.

 Name ____________________

Letter Jj

Say the names of the pictures. Color each picture that begins with the sound of **Jj**.

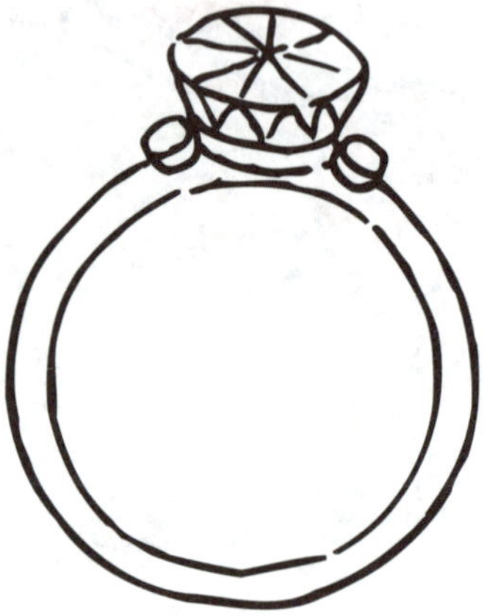

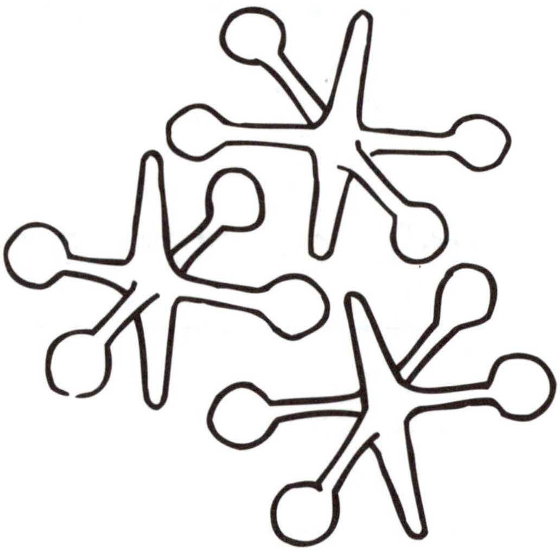

Letter Jj

Help the juggler. Cut out the balls that begin with the sound of **Jj**. Glue them on the balls the juggler is juggling.

Page is blank for cutting exercise on previous page.

Letter Jj

Jim has a ticket for a ride. Color to find the hidden picture.

- Color the spaces with **J** or **j** **blue**.
- Color the other spaces **gray**.

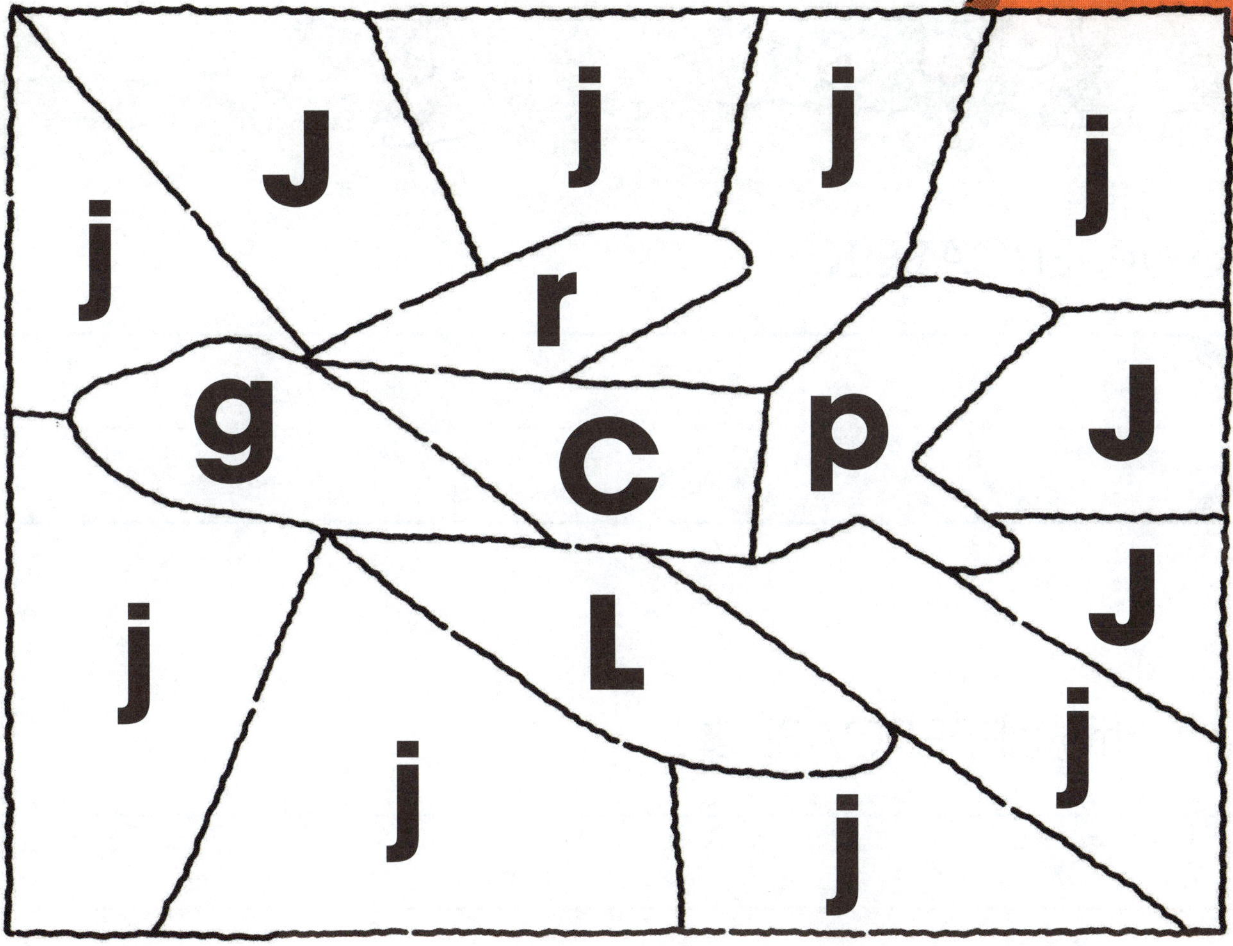

What will Jim ride in? ____________________

Name ______________________

Trace UPPERCASE **K**.

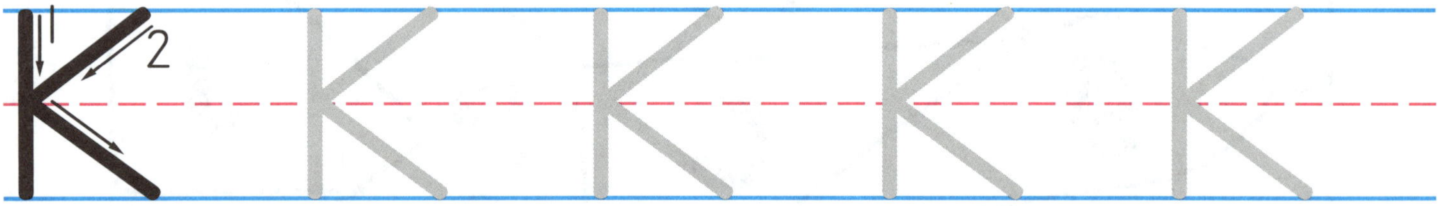

Now, write UPPERCASE **K**.

Trace lowercase **k**.

k k k k k k k

Now, write lowercase **k**.

Name ______________________

Letter Kk

Say the names of the pictures. Color each picture that begins with the sound of **Kk**.

Letter Kk

Look at the letters on each key and lock. Draw a line between the keys and locks with matching letters.

Name ______________________

Letter Kk

Say the names of the pictures on the kites. If a picture begins with the **Kk** sound, draw a kite string from the kite to a child's hand.

Letter Review

Draw a line from each UPPERCASE letter to its matching lowercase letter.

Name ____________________

Trace UPPERCASE **L**.

Now, write UPPERCASE **L**.

Trace lowercase **l**.

Now, write lowercase **l**.

Name ______________________________

Letter Ll

Say the names of the pictures. Color each picture that begins with the sound of **Ll**.

Letter Ll

Climb the ladder by coloring the pictures that begin with the sound of **Ll**.

Name ____________________

Trace UPPERCASE **M**.

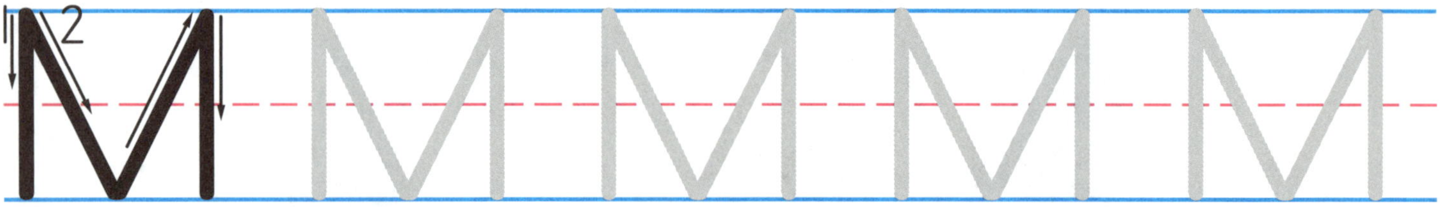

Now, write UPPERCASE **M**.

Trace lowercase **m**.

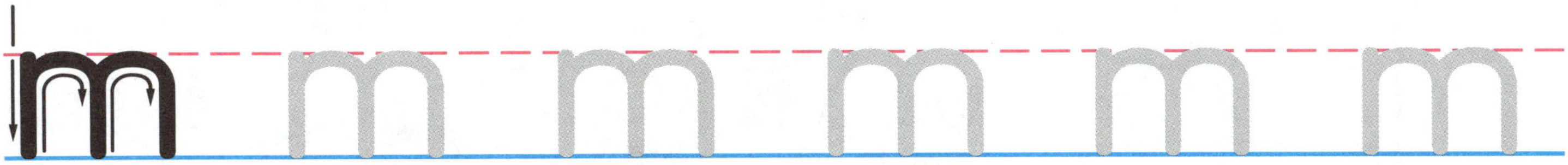

Now, write lowercase **m**.

Name ______________________

Letter Mm

Color to find the hidden picture.

- Color the spaces with **M** **gray**.
- Color the spaces with **m** **yellow**.
- Color the other spaces with a color you like.

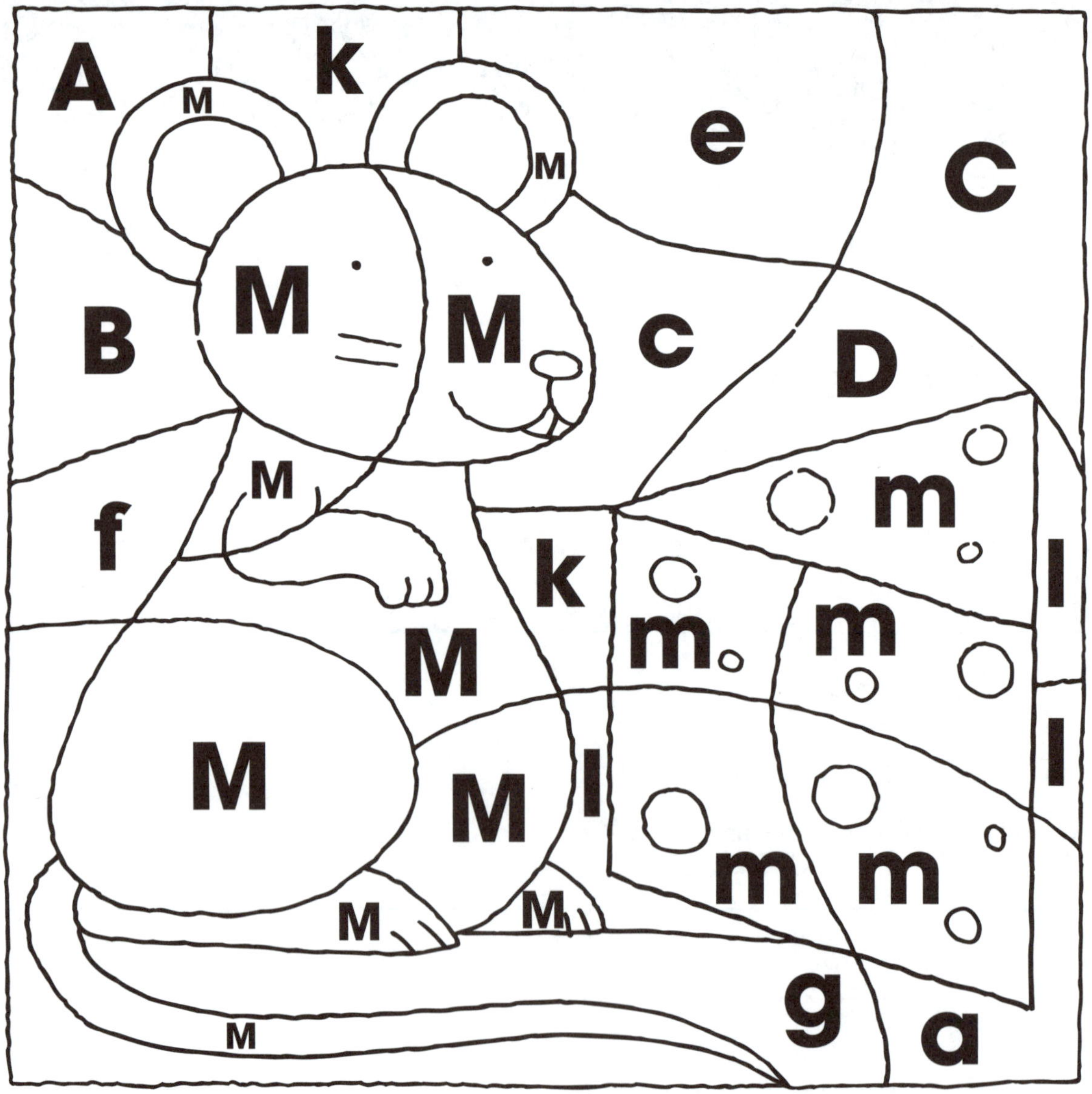

What did you find? ______________________

Letter Mm

Help the mouse get to the cheese. Say the name of each picture. Follow the path of pictures that begin with the sound of **Mm**.

 Name ______________________

Trace UPPERCASE **N**.

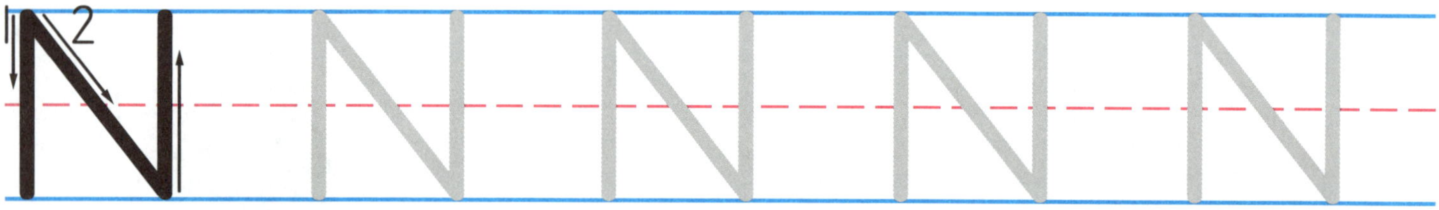

Now, write UPPERCASE **N**.

Trace lowercase **n**.

n n n n n n n

Now, write lowercase **n**.

Name ______________________

Letter Nn

Say the names of the pictures. Color each picture that begins with the sound of **Nn**.

Letter Nn

Cut out the eggs with **N** or **n** on them. Then, glue them in the nest below.

Page is blank for cutting exercise on previous page.

Letter Nn

Draw a line from the letters **Nn** to the pictures that begin with the sound of **Nn**.

Nn

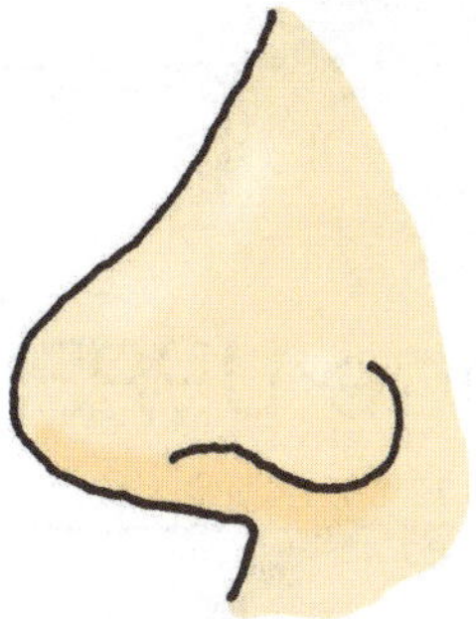

Nn

Nn

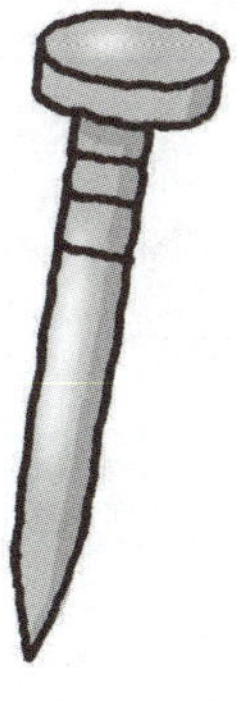

Name ______________________

Trace UPPERCASE **O**.

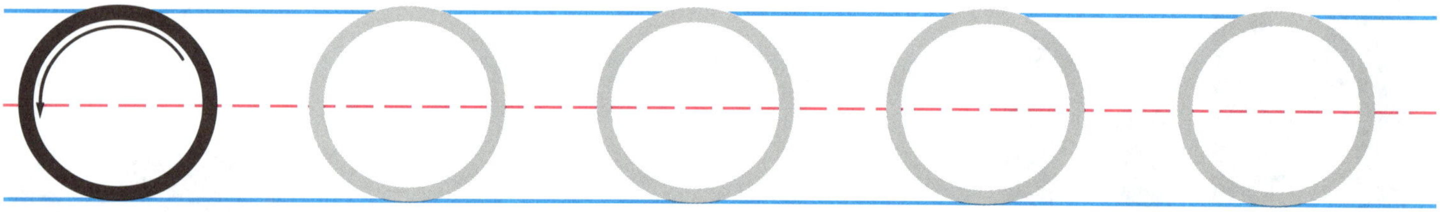

Now, write UPPERCASE **O**.

Trace lowercase **o**.

Now, write lowercase **o**.

Name ______________________

Letter Oo

Say the names of the pictures. Color each picture that begins with the sound of **Oo**.

Letter Oo

What did the octopus see on the ocean floor?

- Color the spaces with **O** or **o** **blue**.
- Color the other spaces **brown**.

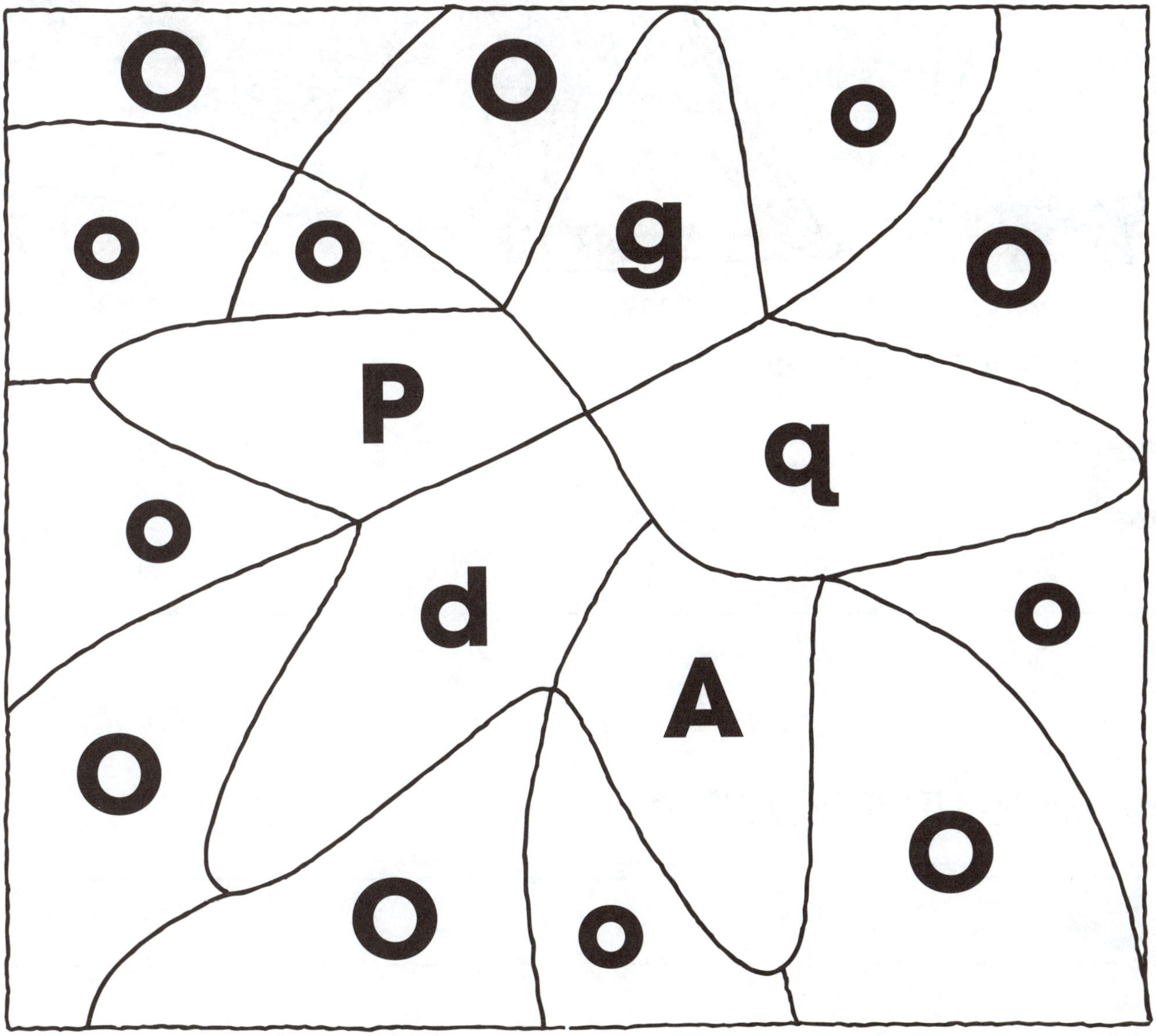

What did the octopus see? ______________________________

Name ____________________

Trace UPPERCASE **P**.

Now, write UPPERCASE **P**.

Trace lowercase **p**.

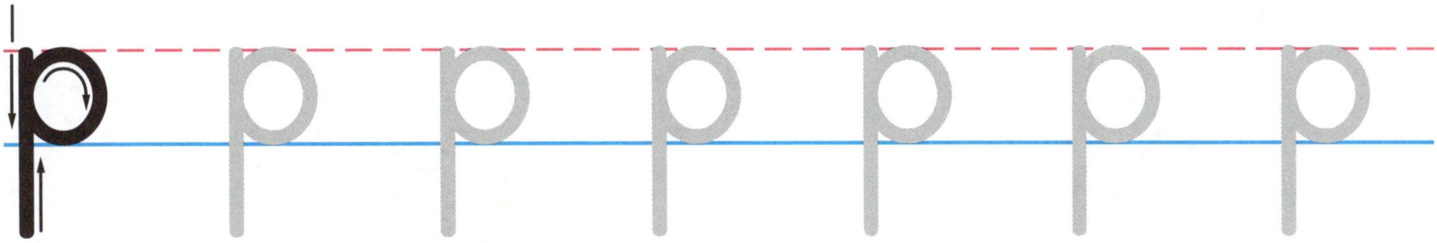

Now, write lowercase **p**.

Name ____________________

Letter Pp

Say the names of the pictures. Color each picture that begins with the sound of **Pp**.

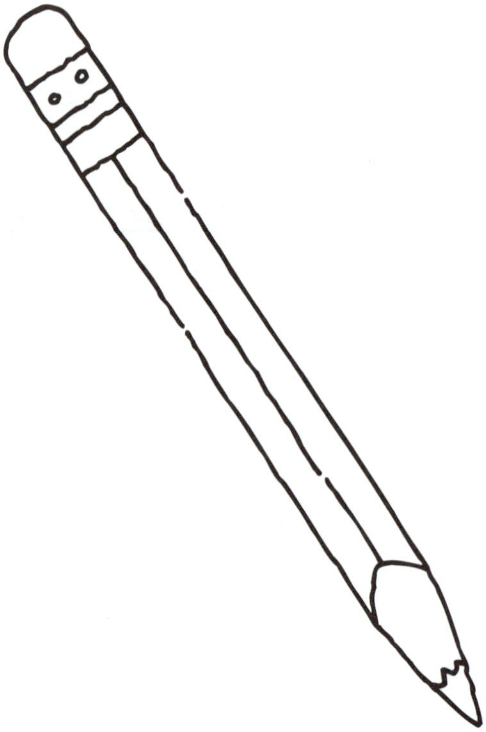

Letter Pp

Cut out the party hats with **P** or **p**. Glue them on the children's heads.

Page is blank for cutting exercise on previous page.

Letter Review

Cut out the letter cards below and on page 283. Match the UPPER- and lowercase letters.

A	a	B	b
C	c	D	d
E	e	F	f
G	g	H	h

Page is blank for cutting exercise on previous page.

Letter Review

I	i	J	j
K	k	L	l
M	m	N	n
O	o	P	p

Page is blank for cutting exercise on previous page.

Letter Review

Connect the dots as you say the alphabet from **A** to **P**. Then, color the picture.

Name ____________________

Trace UPPERCASE **Q**.

Now, write UPPERCASE **Q**.

Trace lowercase **q**.

Now, write lowercase **q**.

Name ______________________________

Letter Qq

Say the names of the pictures. Color each picture that begins with the sound of **Qq**.

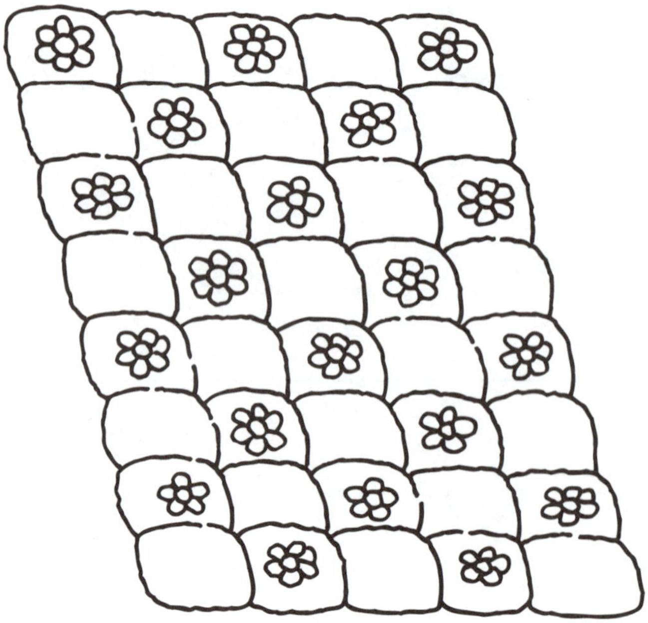

Letter Qq

Help finish the queen's crown. Cut out the rhombuses with the **Qq** sound. Glue them on top of the crown.

Page is blank for cutting exercise on previous page.

Letter Qq

Color the quilt.

- Color the squares with **Q** **green**.
- Color the squares with **q** **pink**.

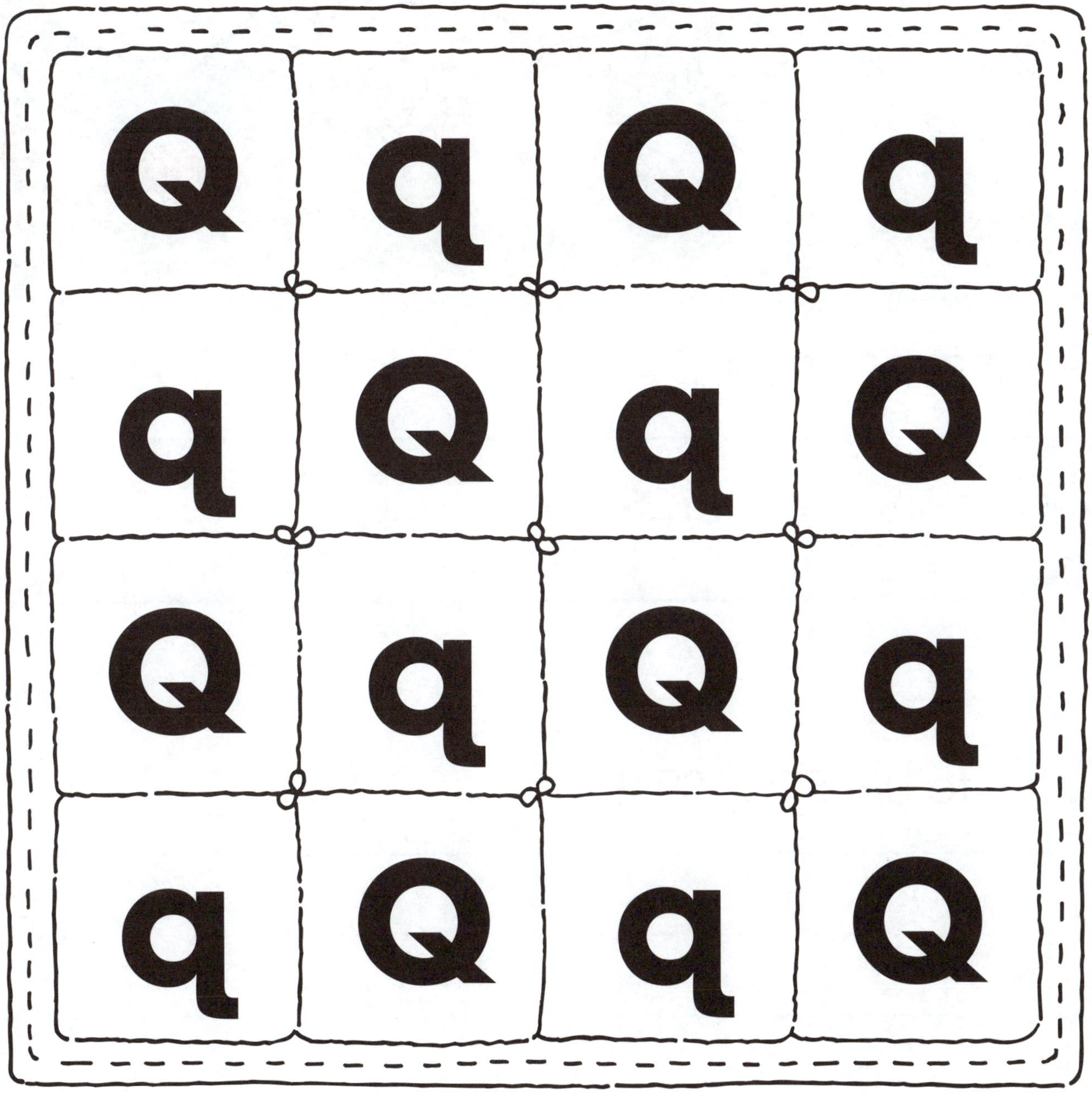

 Name ______________________

Trace UPPERCASE **R**.

R R R R R

Now, write UPPERCASE **R**.

Trace lowercase **r**.

r r r r r r r

Now, write lowercase **r**.

Name ______________________

Letter Rr

Say the names of the pictures. Color each picture that begins with the sound of **Rr**.

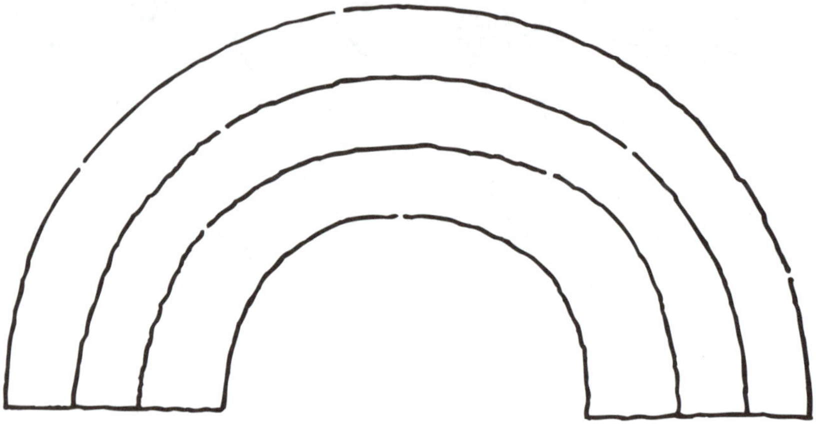

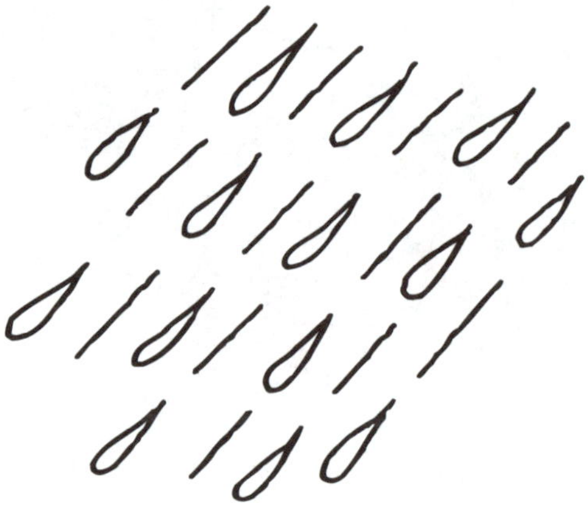

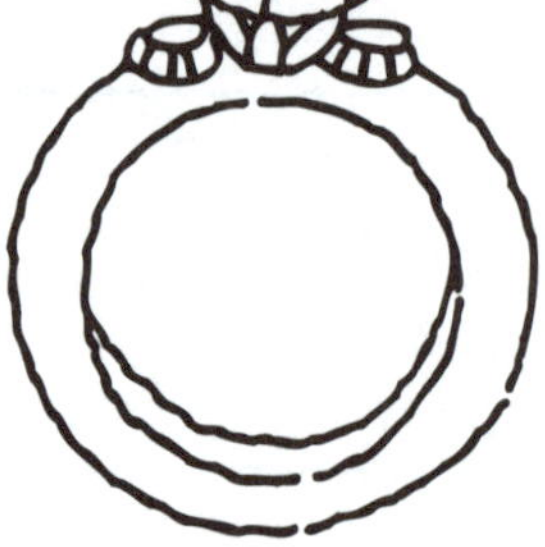

Letter Rr

Help finish the umbrella. Cut out the pieces with **R** or **r** on them. Then, glue them in the correct places.

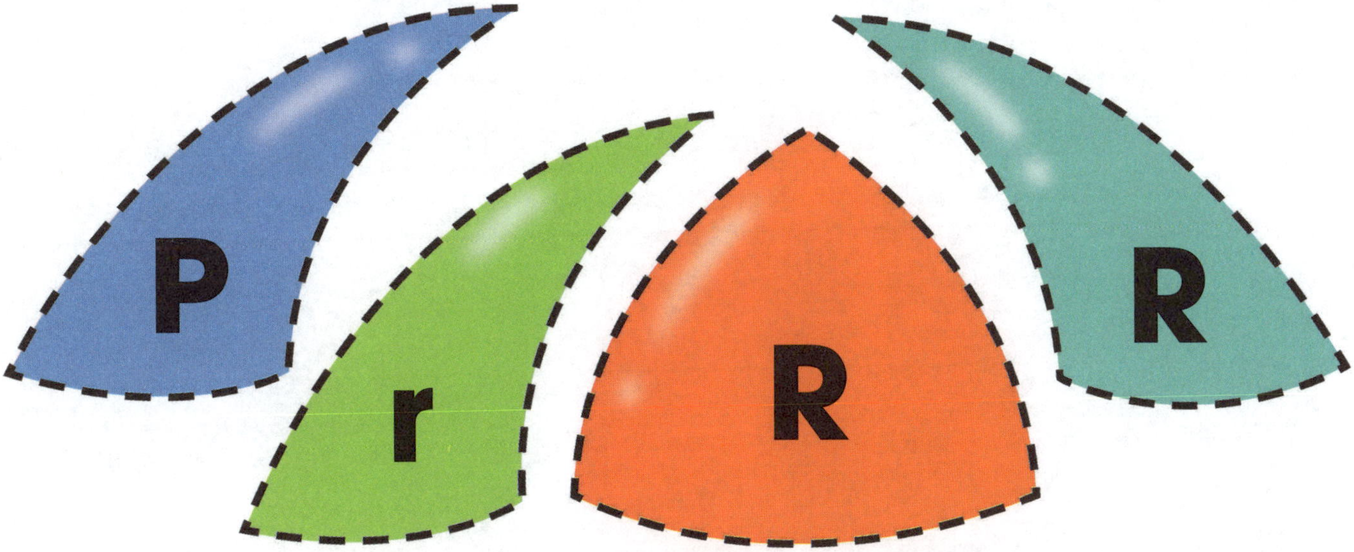

Page is blank for cutting exercise on previous page.

Letter Rr

Draw a line from each **Rr** to an animal whose name begins with the sound of **Rr**.

Rr

Rr

Rr

Name ______________________________

Trace UPPERCASE **S**.

Now, write UPPERCASE **S**.

Trace lowercase **s**.

s s s s s s s

Now, write lowercase **s**.

Name ______________________

Letter Ss

Say the names of the pictures. Color each picture that begins with the sound of **Ss**.

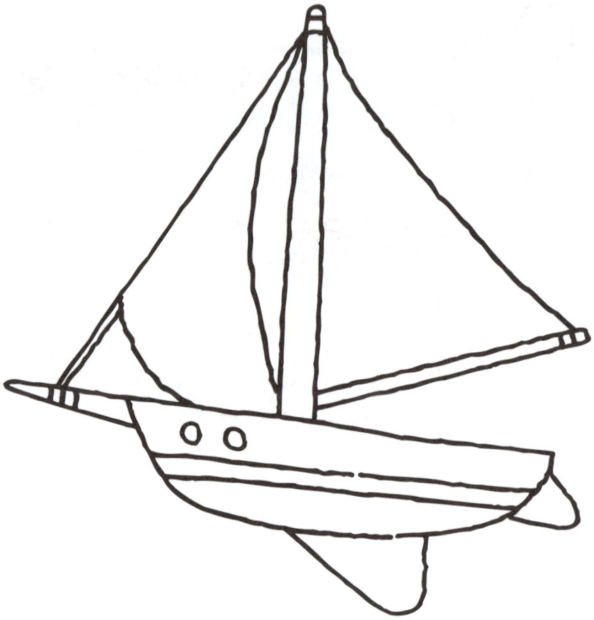

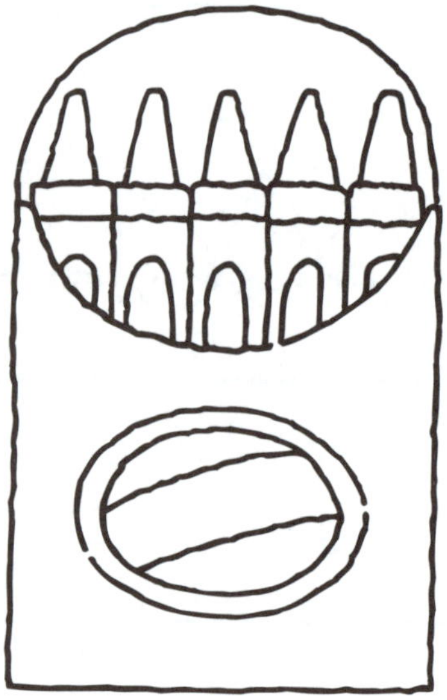

Letter Ss

Look at the letter patterns on the shirts and shorts. Draw a line from each shirt to the pair of shorts with the same letter pattern.

Name ____________________

Trace UPPERCASE **T**.

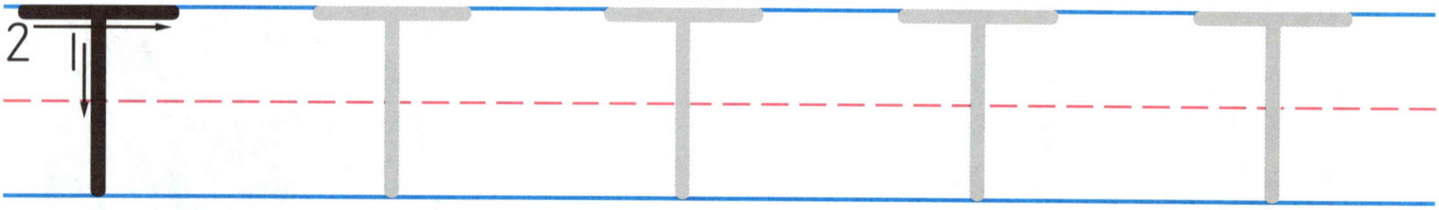

Now, write UPPERCASE **T**.

Trace lowercase **t**.

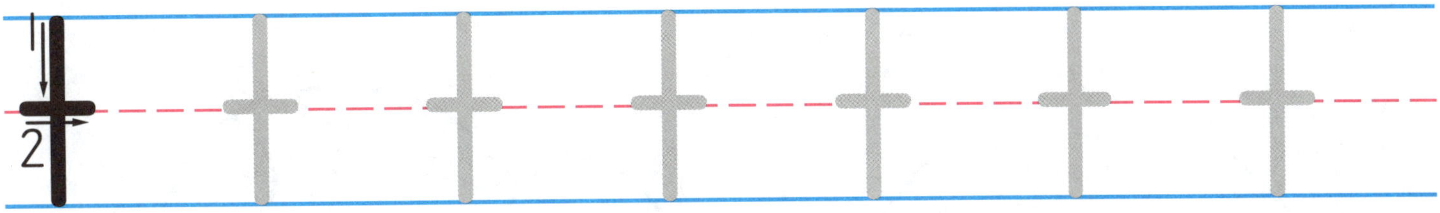

Now, write lowercase **t**.

Name ____________________

Letter Tt

Say the names of the pictures. Color each picture that begins with the sound of **Tt**.

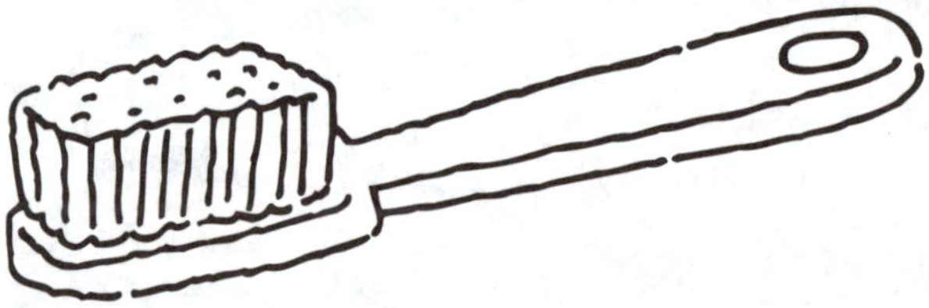

Letter Tt

Trace the letters **T** and **t** on the turkey's feathers below. Then, cut out the feathers and glue them on the turkey.

Page is blank for cutting exercise on previous page.

Letter Tt

Help Taylor and her mom get to the tent for their campout. Follow the path of pictures that begin with the sound of **Tt**.

 Name ______________________

Trace UPPERCASE **U**.

Now, write UPPERCASE **U**.

Trace lowercase **u**.

u u u u u u u

Now, write lowercase **u**.

Name ___________________________

Letter Uu

Say the names of the pictures. Color each picture that begins with the sound of **Uu**.

Letter Uu

Blast off to the moon! Trace the **Uu** letter path to send the rocket up into outer space.

Name ____________________

V

Trace UPPERCASE **V**.

V V V V V

Now, write UPPERCASE **V**.

v

Trace lowercase **v**.

v v v v v v v

Now, write lowercase **v**.

Name ______________________

Letter Vv

Say the names of the pictures. Color each picture that begins with the sound of **Vv**.

Letter Vv

Draw a line from each **Vv** to a picture that begins with the sound of **Vv**.

Vv

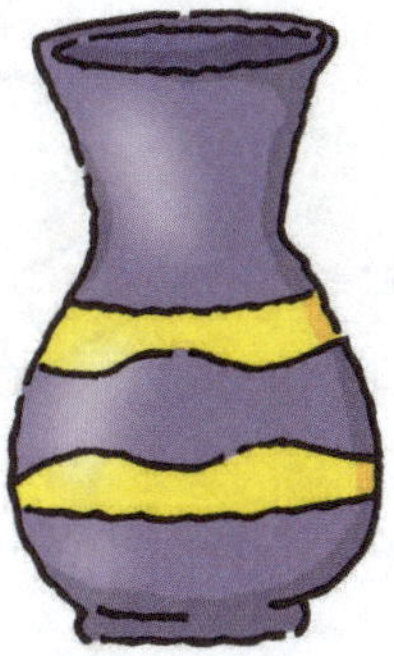

Vv

Vv

Name ______________________

Trace UPPERCASE **W**.

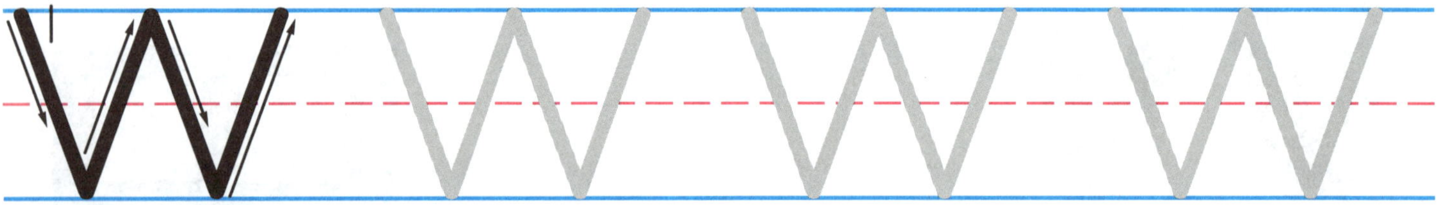

Now, write UPPERCASE **W**.

Trace lowercase **w**.

w w w w w w

Now, write lowercase **w**.

Name ______________________

Letter Ww

Say the names of the pictures. Color each picture that begins with the sound of **Ww**.

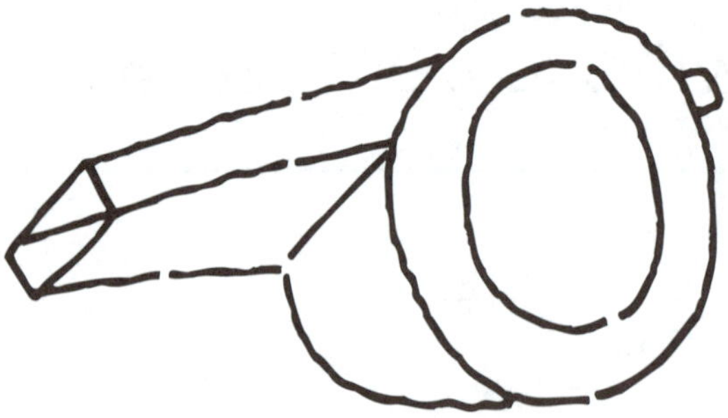

Letter Ww

Help hang up the wash. Cut out the pictures that begin with the sound of **Ww**. Then, glue them on the clothesline.

Page is blank for cutting exercise on previous page.

Letter Ww

Find the things in the picture that begin with the sound of **Ww**. Then, circle them.

Name ______________________

Letter Review

Help feed the hungry walruses. Draw a line from each UPPERCASE letter to its matching lowercase letter.

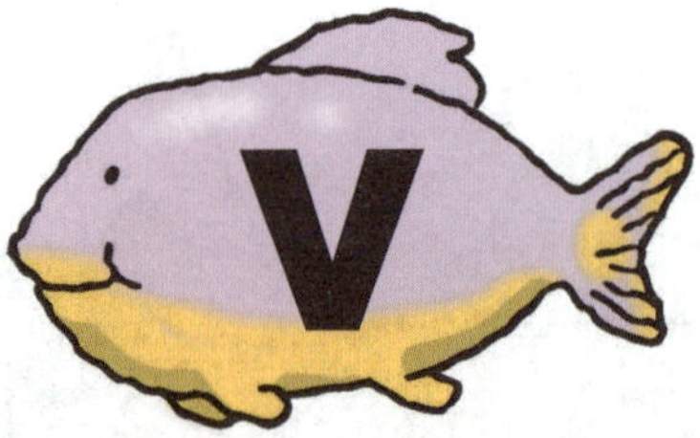

Letter Review

Connect the dots as you say the alphabet from **A** to **W**. Then, color the picture.

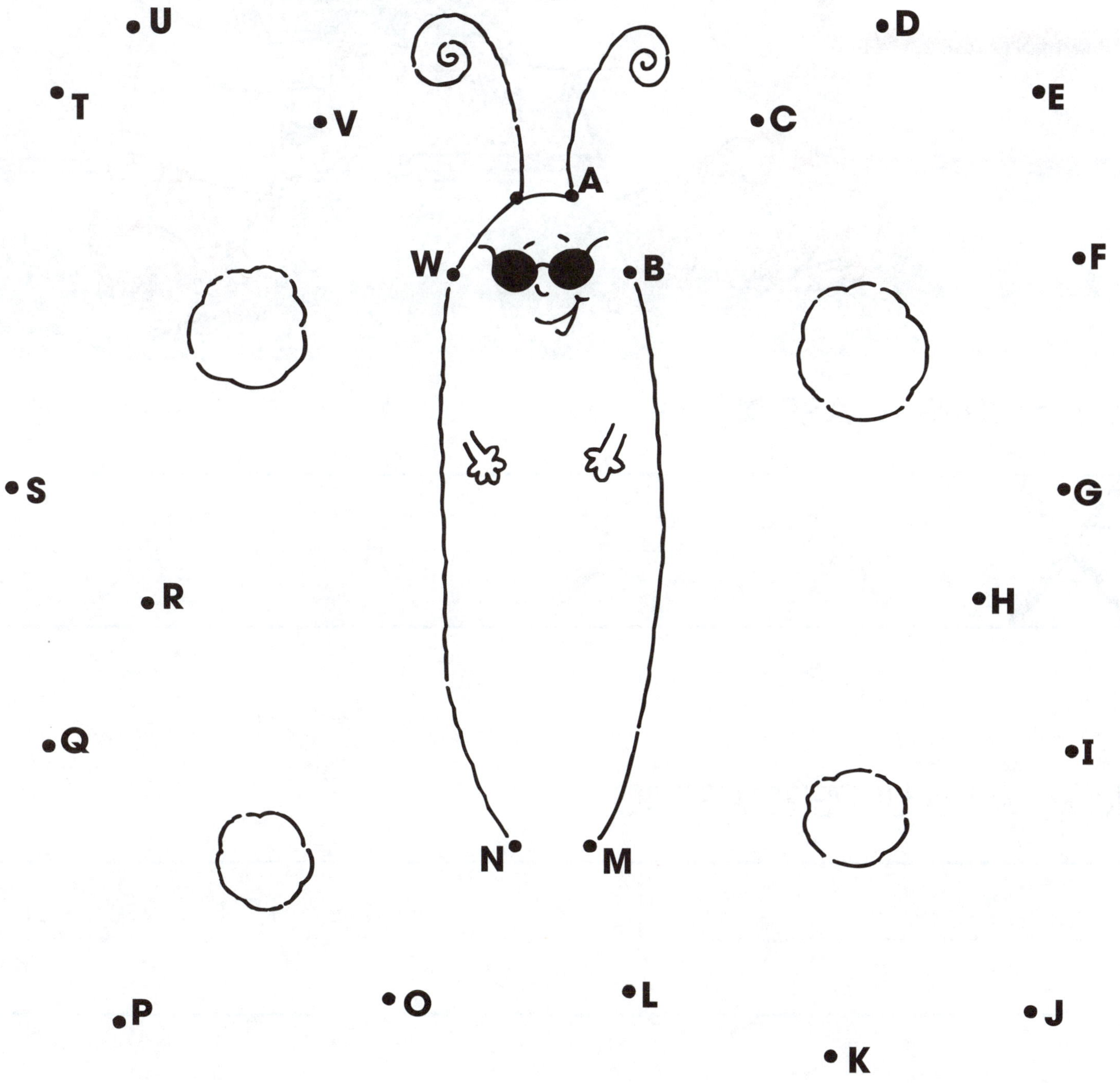

Name ________________

Trace UPPERCASE **X**.

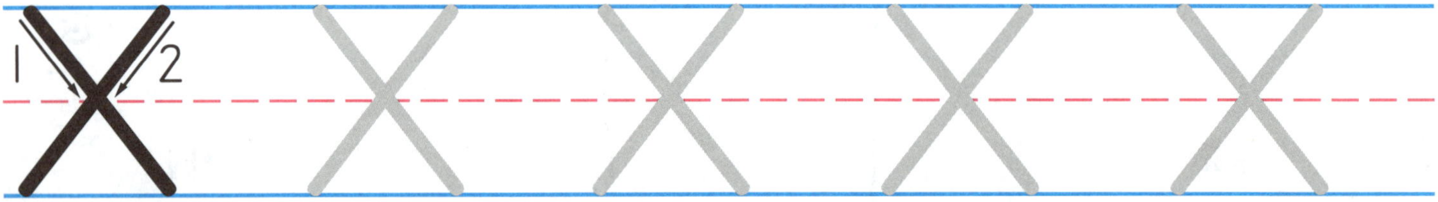

Now, write UPPERCASE **X**.

Trace lowercase **x**.

1 2
x x x x x x x

Now, write lowercase **x**.

Name ______________________

Letter Xx

Say the names of the pictures. Color each picture that begins with the sound of **Xx**.

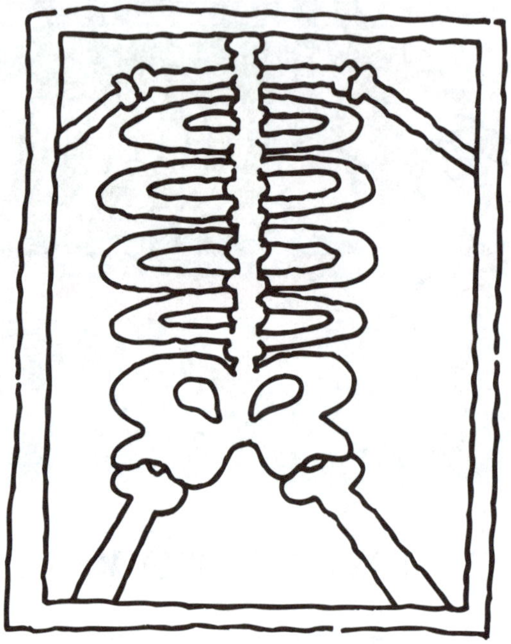

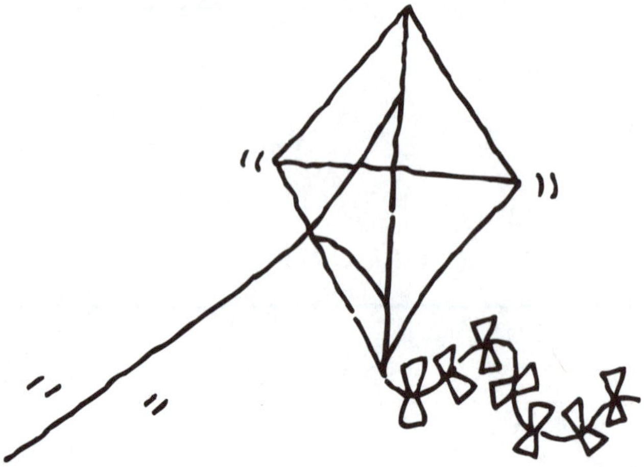

Letter Xx

Say the names of the pictures below. Then, trace the **x** to complete each word.

fox

box

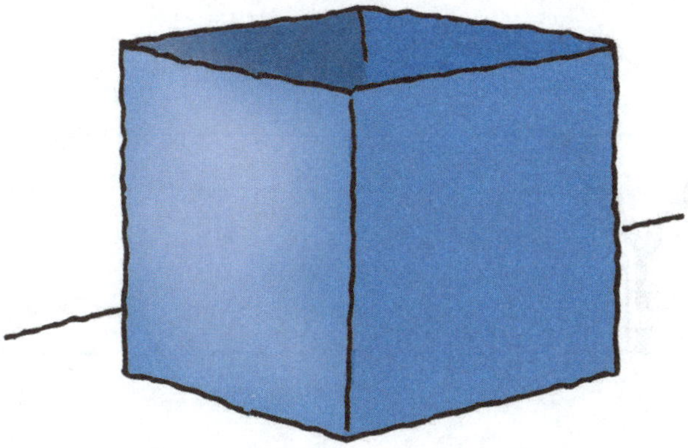

ox

Name ______________________

Trace UPPERCASE **Y**.

Now, write UPPERCASE **Y**.

Trace lowercase **y**.

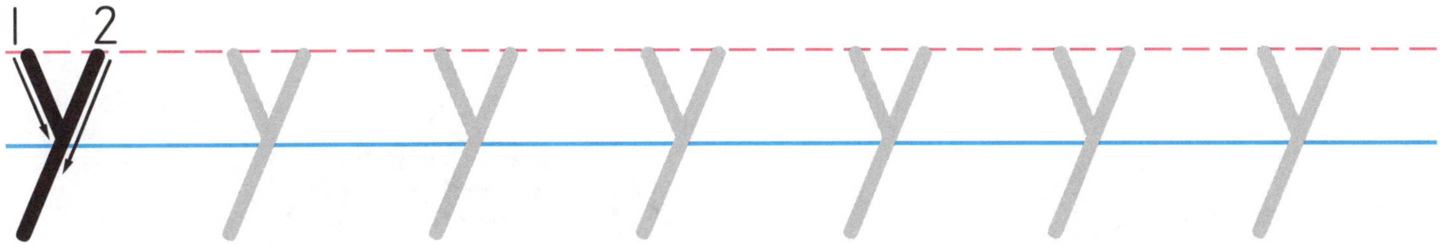

Now, write lowercase **y**.

Letter Yy

Say the names of the pictures. Color each picture that begins with the sound of **Yy**.

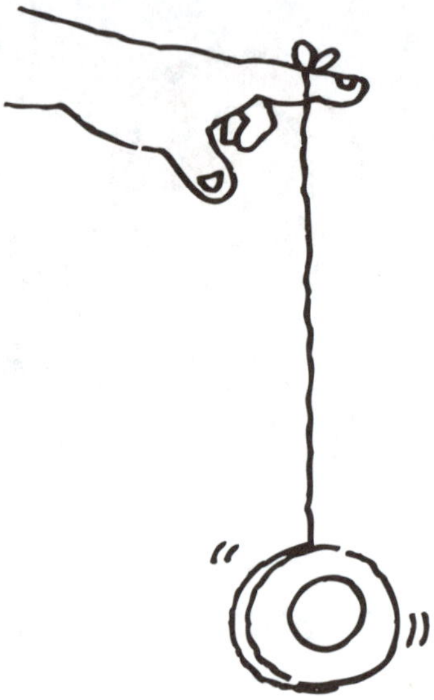

Letter Yy

Color to find the hidden picture.

- Color the spaces with **Y** **yellow**.
- Color the other spaces **orange**.

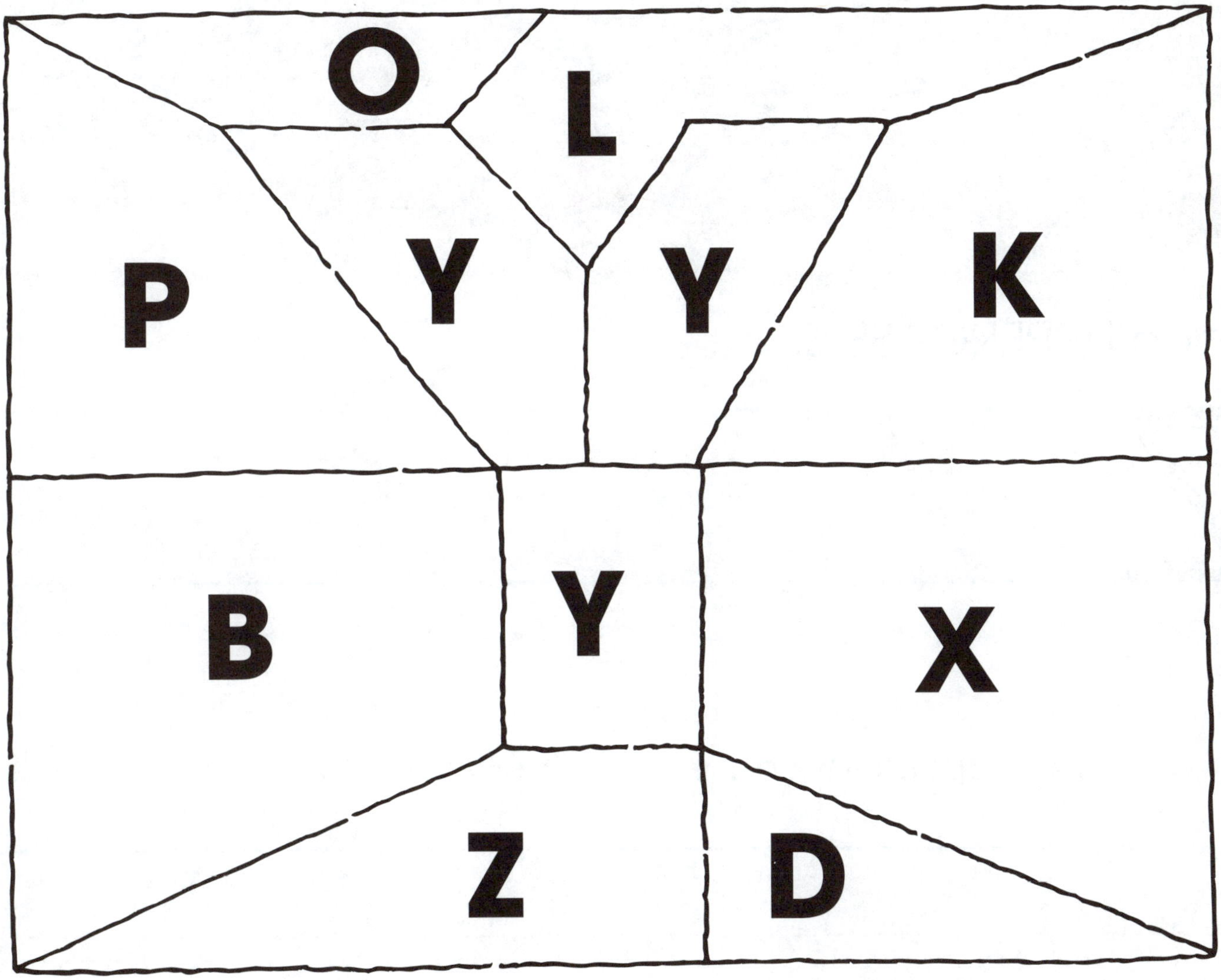

What did you find? ______________________________

Name ____________________

Trace UPPERCASE **Z**.

Z Z Z Z Z

Now, write UPPERCASE **Z**.

Name ____________________

Trace lowercase **z**.

z z z z z z z

Now, write lowercase **z**.

Name ____________________

Letter Zz

Say the names of the pictures. Color each picture that begins with the sound of **Zz**.

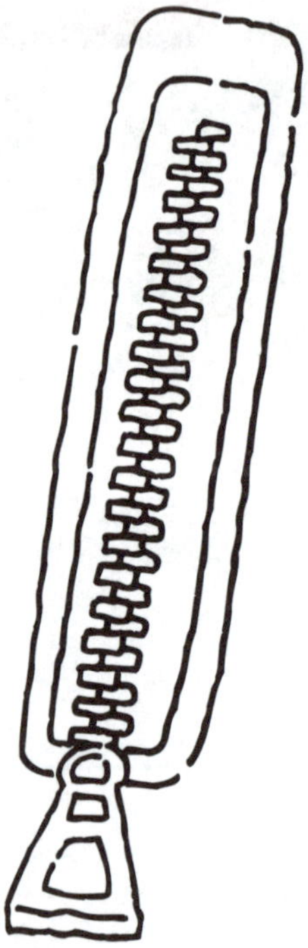

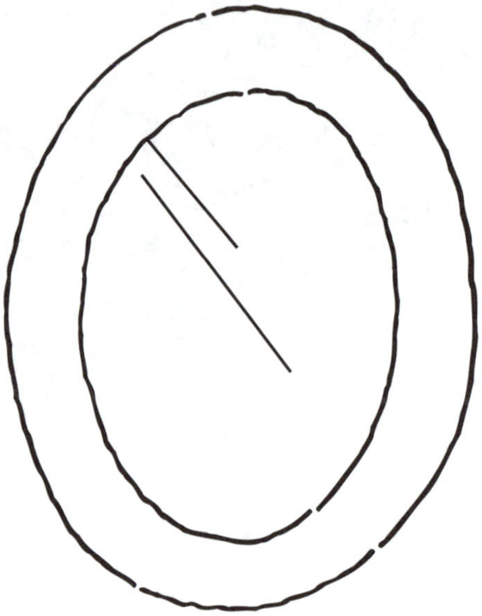

Letter Zz

These zippers need zipper pulls. Cut out the pictures below that begin with **Zz**. Then, glue them on the zipper pulls.

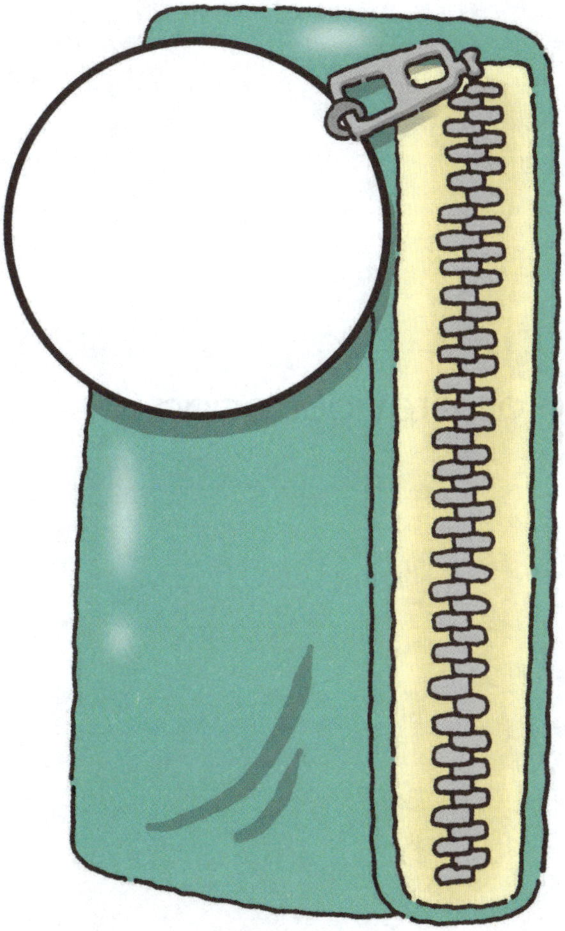

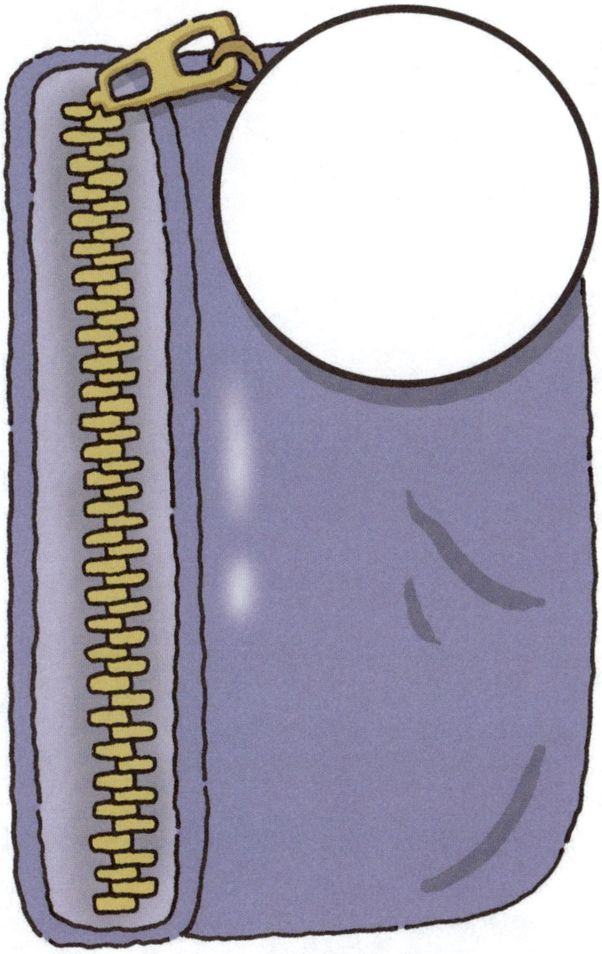

Page is blank for cutting exercise on previous page.

Letter Review

Cut out the letter cards below and on page 339.
Match the UPPER- and lowercase letters.

Q	q	R	r
S	s	T	t
U	u	V	v
W	w	X	x

Page is blank for cutting exercise on previous page.

Letter Review

Y y Z z

Page is blank for cutting exercise on previous page.

Letter Review

Cut out the alphabet cards below and on pages 343-353. Use them to practice your ABCs.

Aa

Bb

Cc

Dd

Page is blank for cutting exercise on previous page.

Letter Review

Ee

Ff

Gg

Hh

Page is blank for cutting exercise on previous page.

Letter Review

Page is blank for cutting exercise on previous page.

Letter Review

Mm

Nn

Oo

Pp

Page is blank for cutting exercise on previous page.

Letter Review

Page is blank for cutting exercise on previous page.

Letter Review

Uu

Vv

Ww

Xx

Page is blank for cutting exercise on previous page.

Letter Review

Page is blank for cutting exercise on previous page.

Letter Review

Practice writing the letters A-Z below and on pages 356 and 357. Trace the UPPER- and lowercase letters.

Aa Bb Cc

Dd Ee Ff

Gg Hh Ii

Name ____________________

Letter Review

Jj Kk Ll

Mm Nn Oo

Pp Qq Rr

Letter Review

Ss Tt Uu

Vv Ww Xx

Yy Zz

Name ______________________________

Beginning Sounds

Look at the pictures in each row. Circle the sound each picture begins with. Then, color the pictures.

s n p | d g b

t r l | h s m

Beginning Sounds

Look at the pictures in each row. Color the picture that has the same beginning sound as the first picture.

Name ____________________

Beginning Sounds

Look at the pictures in each row. Color two pictures in each row that begin with the same sound.

Beginning Sounds

Draw a line from each letter to the picture that begins with that sound.

m

g

o

Name ______________________

Beginning Sounds

Draw a line from each letter to the picture that begins with that sound.

v

z

b

Beginning Sounds

Draw a line from each letter to the picture that begins with that sound.

s

y

h

Name ______________________

Beginning Sounds

Draw a line from each letter to the picture that begins with that sound.

a

j

t

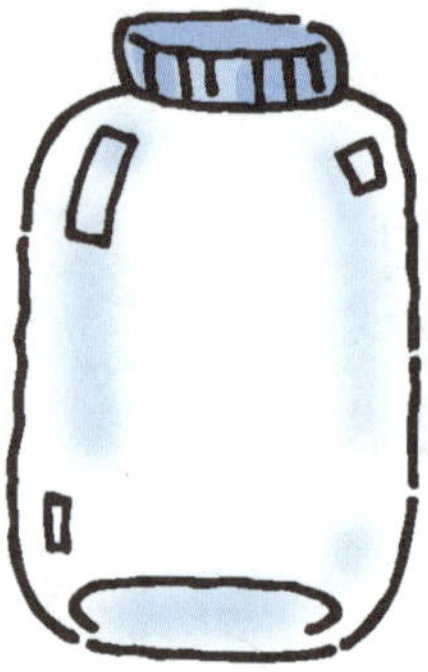

Rhyming Pictures

Look at the pictures in each row. Color the picture that rhymes with the first picture.

Name ____________________

Rhyming Pictures

Look at the pictures in each row. Color the picture that rhymes with the first picture.

Rhyming Pictures

Look at the pictures in each row. Color the picture that rhymes with the first picture.

Name ______________________

Rhyming Pictures

Look at the pictures below. Draw lines to match the rhyming pictures.

Rhyming Pictures

Look at the pictures below. Draw lines to match the rhyming pictures.

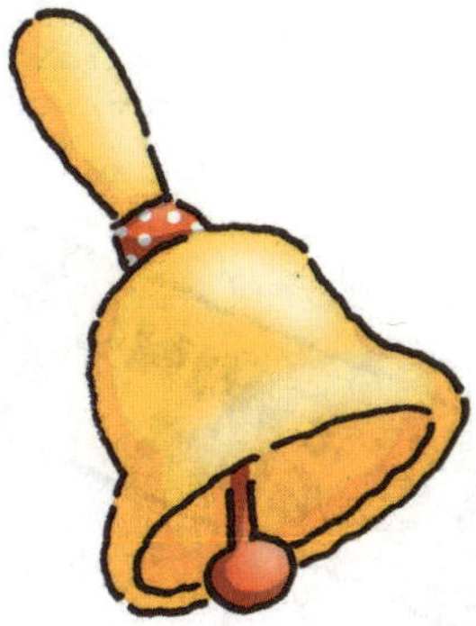

Name ___________________________

Rhyming Pictures

Look at the pictures below. Draw lines to match the rhyming pictures.

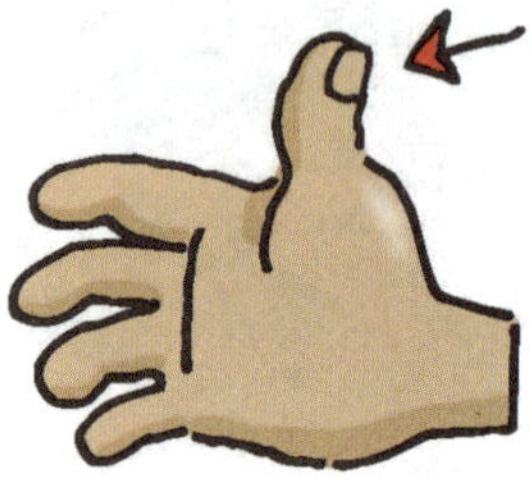

MATHEMATICS READINESS

Name ______________________

Trace the number **0**.

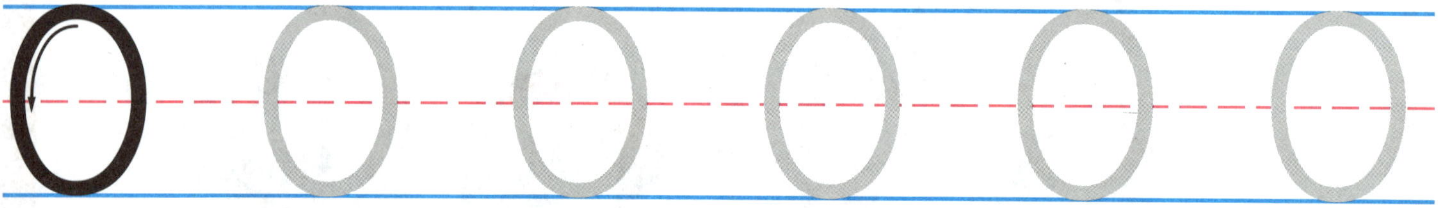

Now, write the number **0**.

Trace the word **zero**.

zero zero zero

Now, write the word **zero**.

Name ______________________________

0 zero

Color the fish with **0** spots orange.

0 zero

Circle the fishbowls with **0** fish in them. Write **0** on the line beside them.

 ______

 ______

 ______

 ______

Name ______________________

Trace the number 1.

Now, write the number 1.

Trace the word **one**.

one one one

Now, write the word **one**.

Name ______________________

1 one

Circle 1 picture in each box. Then, write the number 1 on the line in each box.

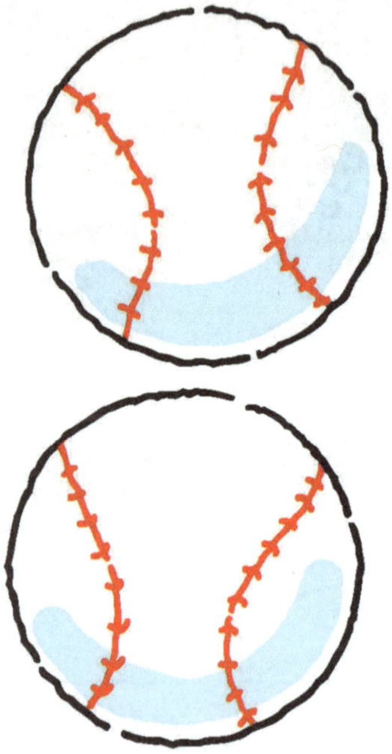

______

______

______

______

I one

Draw a line to match each number **I** to one thing.

I

I

I

Name ______________________

Trace the number **2**.

2 2 2 2 2 2

Now, write the number **2**.

Trace the word **two**.

two two two

Now, write the word **two**.

Name ______________________________

2 two

Draw a line to match each number **2** to a group of **2** things.

2

2

2

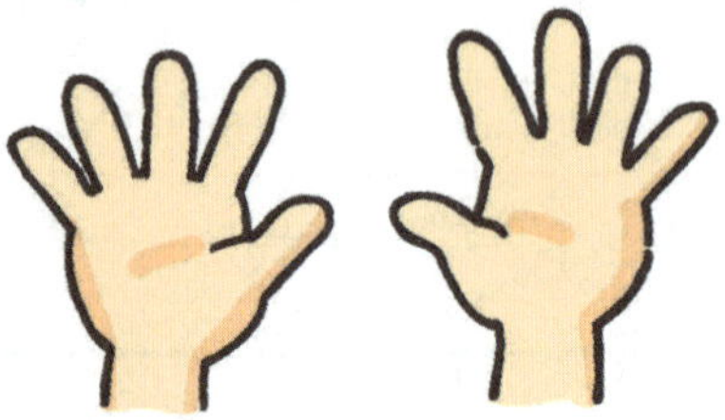

2 two

Draw another picture in each box to make **2** of each thing.

Name ______________________

2 two

Color to find something that comes in twos.

- Color the spaces with **2** **yellow**.
- Color the spaces with **1** **blue**.

What did you find? ______________________

2 two

Circle **2** pictures in each box. Then, write the number **2** on the line in each box.

______

______

______

______

Name ______________________________

Trace the number **3**.

3 3 3 3 3 3

Now, write the number **3**.

Trace the word **three**.

three three

Now, write the word **three**.

Name ______________________

3 three

Draw to complete each pattern of **3**.

3 three

Circle **3** of each kind of cookies to go in the cookie jar.

Name ____________________

3 three

Count the number of pictures in each box. Circle the number that tells how many there are.

1 2 3

1 2 3

1 2 3

1 2 3

3 three

Draw pictures so there are **3** things in each box. Then, write a **3** on the line in each box.

______

______

______

______

Name ____________________

Trace the number **4**.

Now, write the number **4**.

four

Trace the word **four**.

four four four

Now, write the word **four**.

Name ______________________________

4 four

Count the flowers in each group. Circle the number that tells how many there are.

2 3 4

2 3 4

2 3 4

2 3 4

4 four

Count the leaves on each flower. Draw more leaves so there are **4** on each stem. Trace and write **4** on the lines below.

Name ___________________________

4 four

Draw **4** flowers in the vase.

4 four

Color to find the hidden picture.

- Color the spaces with **2** **blue**.
- Color the spaces with **3** **blue**.
- Color the spaces with **4** **green**.

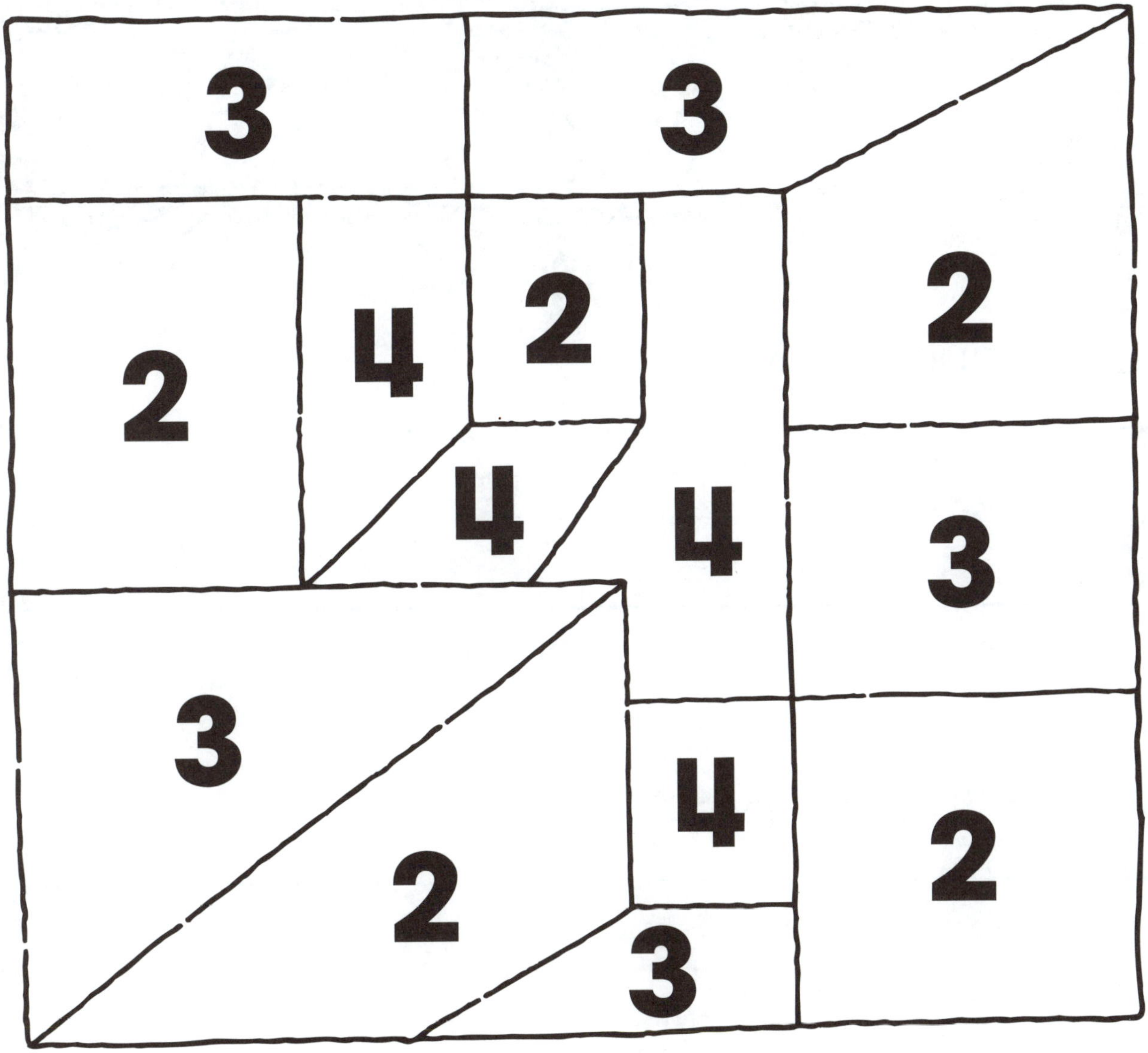

What did you find? ______________________

Name ____________________

Trace the number **5**.

5 5 5 5 5 5

Now, write the number **5**.

five

Trace the word **five**.

five five five

Now, write the word **five**.

Name ____________________

5 five

Count how many there are in each group. Circle the number that tells how many there are.

5 five

Count the shapes in each box. Draw more so that each box has **5** shapes in it. Write **5** on each line.

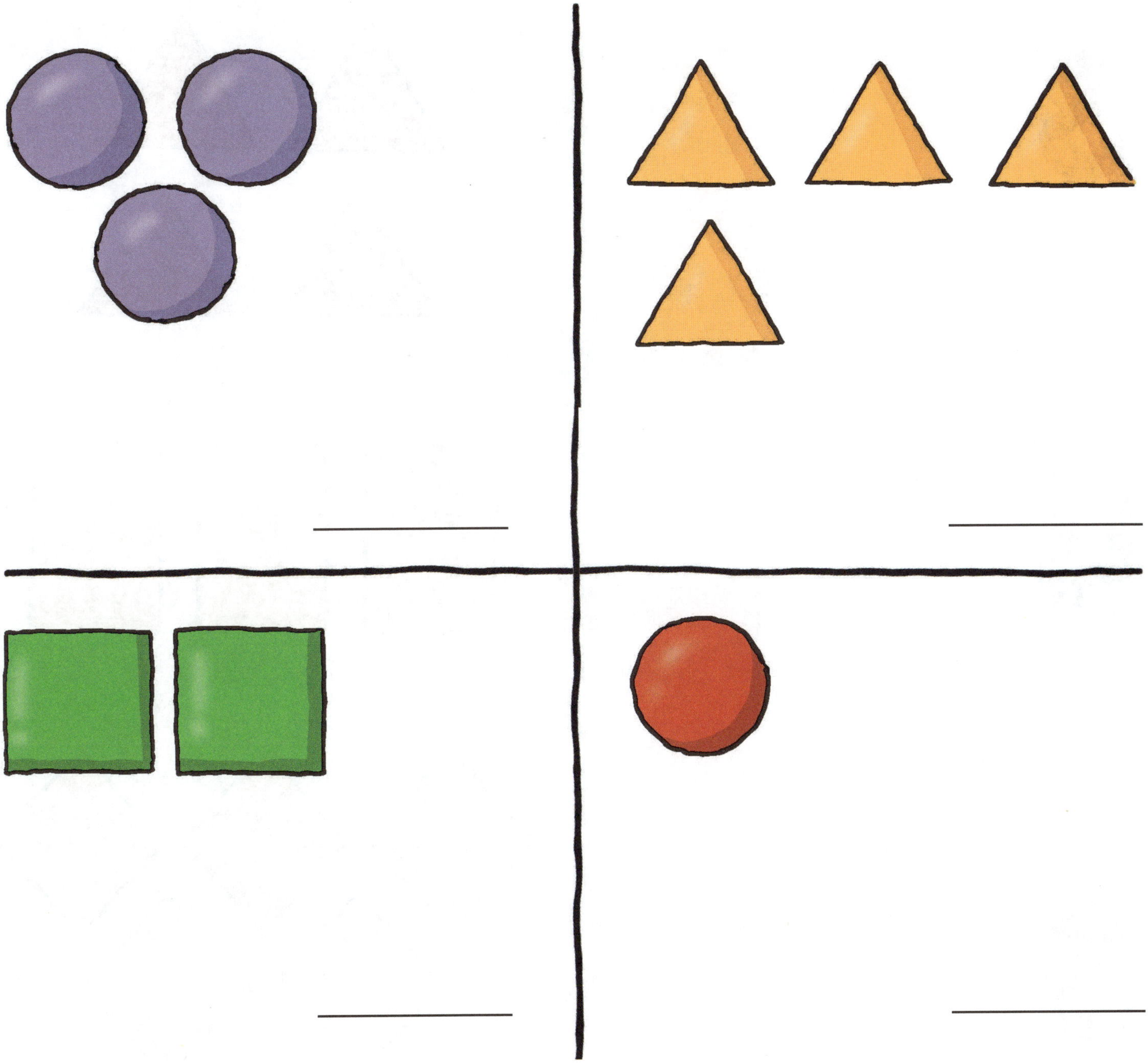

Name ______________________________

5 five

Draw a line to match each number to the group that has the same number of shapes.

3

4

5

5 five

Count the shapes. Then, color and decorate the butterfly.

How many ○'s? __________

How many △'s? __________ How many ▭'s? __________

Name ____________________

1-5 Review

Count the fish in each group. Write the number that tells how many there are.

1-5 Review

Draw a line to match each number to the group that has that many things in it.

2

3

4

5

Name ____________________

I-5 Review

Trace and write the missing numbers below.

1 2 3 4 5

4 5

1

1-5 Review

Follow the directions to color the picture below.

- Color **5** fish **orange**.
- Color **3** fish **brown**.
- Draw **2** **pink** shells.
- Draw **1** **yellow** starfish.

Name ______________________

Trace the number **6**.

Now, write the number **6**.

six

Trace the word **six**.

six six six six

Now, write the word **six**.

Name ____________________

6 six

Circle **6** things in each box. Write the number **6** on each line.

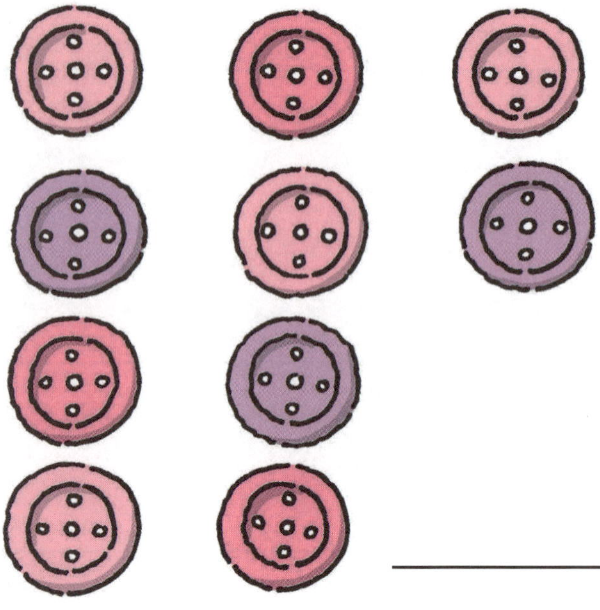

6 six

Count the number of dots on each gas pump. Write the number on the line above each car.

____

____

____

____

Name ________________

6 six

Help the car get to the gas pump. Use a crayon to follow the path of **6**'s.

6 six

Trace the wheels on the unicycle, bicycle, and tricycle. Count the number of wheels you traced. Write the number on each line.

Name ___________________________

Trace the number **7**.

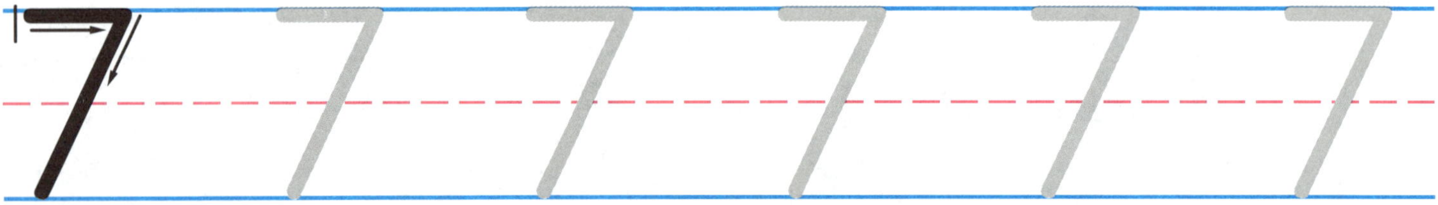

Now, write the number **7**.

Trace the word **seven**.

seven seven

Now, write the word **seven**.

Name ____________________

7 seven

Circle **7** things on each shelf.

7 seven

Count the peanuts in each box. Write the number that tells how many there are.

Name ______________________

7 seven

Color the picture to find a special treat.

- Color the spaces with **5** **green**.
- Color the space with **6** **brown**.
- Color the spaces with **7** **pink**.

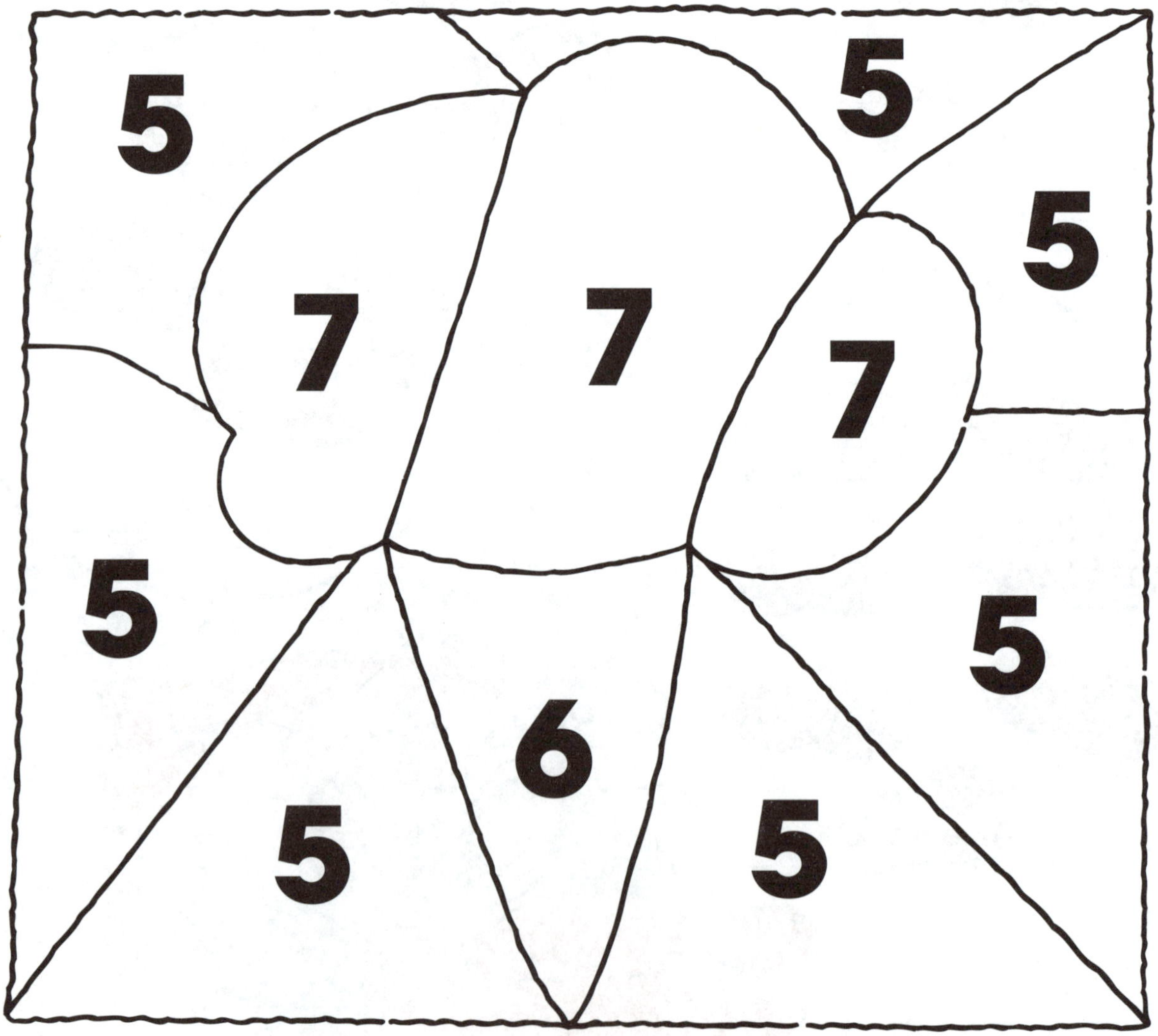

What did you find? ______________________

7 seven

Add some toppings to the pizza.

- Draw **7** pieces of pepperoni.
- Draw **7** mushrooms.

Name ______________________

Trace the number **8**.

Now, write the number **8**.

Trace the word **eight**.

eight eight

Now, write the word **eight**.

Name ______________________

8 eight

Count the things in each box. Write the number that tells how many there are.

8 eight

Draw a line from each basket to the tree with the same number of apples.

Name ___________________________

8 eight

Turn these **8** shoes into pairs. Draw a line to match each shoe on the left with a shoe that is the same on the right.

8 eight

Count and circle **8** legs on each caterpillar.

Name ______________________

Trace the number **9**.

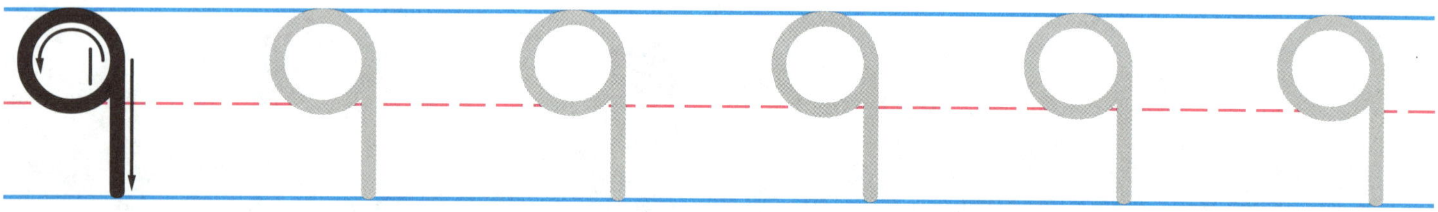

Now, write the number **9**.

nine

Trace the word **nine**.

nine nine nine

Now, write the word **nine**.

Name ______________________________

9 nine

Circle 9 bugs in each group.

9 nine

Read the number on each bee. Draw a line from each bee to the flower with the same number of petals.

Name ______________________

9 nine

Help the bee get to the flower. Follow the path of numbers from 1 to 9.

9 nine

Draw 9 black dots on the ladybug's back.

Name ______________________________

10

Trace the number **10**.

10 10 10 10

Now, write the number **10**.

ten

Trace the word **ten**.

ten ten ten

Now, write the word **ten**.

Name ____________________

10 ten

Count the number of things in each row. Write the number that tells how many there are.

____

____

____

10 ten

Draw **10** legs on the caterpillar.

Name ______________________________

10 ten

Draw **10** leaves on the branches for the caterpillar to eat.

10 ten

Follow the directions to color the butterfly.

- Color **5** dots **red**.
- Color **3** dots **blue**.
- Color **2** dots **orange**.

Count the dots on the butterfly.
How many are there altogether? ______________________________

Name ____________________

6-10 Review

Connect the dots from **1** to **10** to find a circus treat. Then, color the picture.

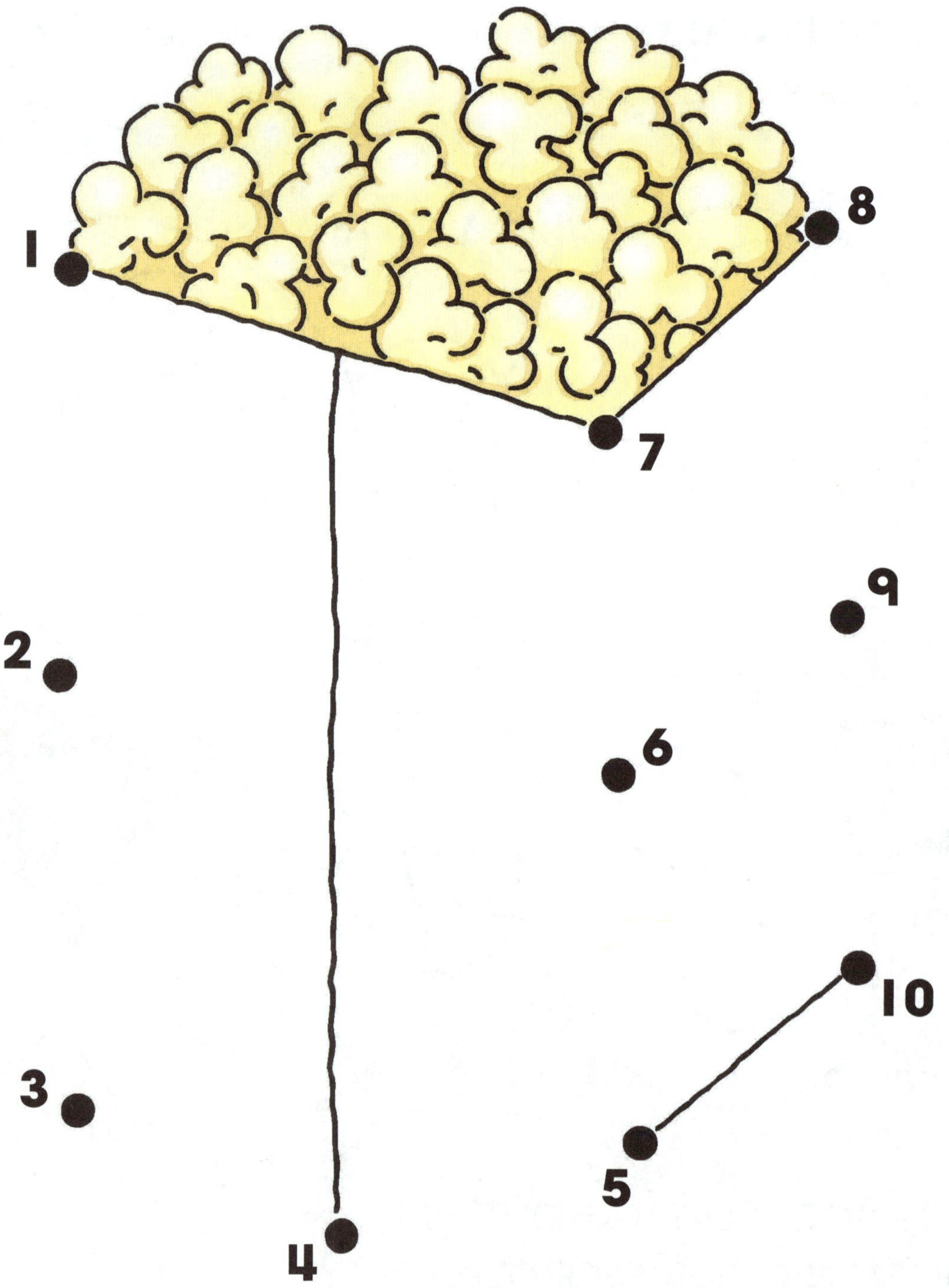

Number Match Game

Cut out the cards below and on pages 441 to 449. Then, match the number cards with the cards that have the same number of dots.

Page is blank for cutting exercise on previous page.

Number Match Game

2

3

Page is blank for cutting exercise on previous page.

Number Match Game

Page is blank for cutting exercise on previous page.

Number Match Game

Page is blank for cutting exercise on previous page.

Number Match Game

Page is blank for cutting exercise on previous page.

Number Match Game

Page is blank for cutting exercise on previous page.

Next

Look at the big picture below. Then, look at the small pictures. Circle the small picture that shows what will happen **next**.

Name ____________________

First, Next, Last

Number the pictures below to show what happened **first**, **next**, and **last**.

- Write **1** under the picture that happened **first**.
- Write **2** under the picture that happened **next**.
- Write **3** under the picture that happened **last**.

__________ __________ __________

First, Next, Last

Number the pictures below to show what happened **first**, **next**, and **last**.

- Write **1** under the picture that happened **first**.
- Write **2** under the picture that happened **next**.
- Write **3** under the picture that happened **last**.

______ ______ ______

 Name ____________________

Ordinal Numbers

Circle the **third** person in line. Draw a line under the **second** person.

Draw an **X** on the **first** person on the bench. Draw a hat on the **fifth** person.

Ordinal Numbers

Draw an **X** on the **fifth** tree. Draw a box around the **third** tree.

Draw a line under the **second** tree. Circle the **first** tree.

Name ______________________

Ordinal Numbers

Circle the **second** box. Draw a green line under the **fifth** box.

Draw red dots on the **third** box. Draw a yellow bow on the **fourth** box.

One-to-One Correspondence

Each dog needs a bone. Trace the line from each dog to its bone.

Name ______________________

One-to-One Correspondence

Draw a line from each rabbit to a carrot. Draw a carrot for the rabbit that does not have one.

One-to-One Correspondence

Trace the string from the cat to the ball of yarn. Then, draw more balls of yarn so each cat has one to play with.

Name ___________________________

More and Fewer

Count the blocks each child is playing with. Circle the child who has **more** blocks.

More and Fewer

Count the blocks in each group. Circle the group of blocks that has **more**.

Name ______________________________

More and Fewer

Count the blocks in the first box. Then, draw a group of blocks that has **more**.

More and Fewer

Count the cars each child is playing with. Circle the child who has **fewer** cars.

Name ______________________

Patterns

Complete the shape patterns. At the end of the row, draw the shape that comes next. Then, color the shape.

____

____

____

Patterns

Complete the picture patterns. At the end of the row, draw the picture that comes next.

____

____

____

Name ____________________

Patterns

Complete the picture patterns. Draw what is missing on the last picture in each row.

Name ____________________

Patterns

Complete the letter patterns. At the end of the row, write the letter that comes next.

C O C O C ______

B P B P B ______

M N M N M ______

Name ______________________

Patterns

Complete the letter patterns. At the end of the row, write the letter that comes next.

L L H L L ______

V V X V V ______

B B D B B ______

Page 10

Draw something else that is **red**.

Drawing will vary.

Now, trace the word **red**.

red

Page 11

Page 12

Draw something else that is **yellow**.

Drawing will vary.

Now, trace the word **yellow**.

yellow

Page 13

Page 14

Draw something else that is **blue**.

Drawing will vary.

Now, trace the word **blue**.

blue

Page 15

Page 16

Page 17

Page 18

Page 19

Page 20

Page 21

Page 22

Page 23

Page 24

Page 25

Page 26

Page 27

WHITE

Color the pictures **white**.

Page 28

Draw something else that is **white**.

Drawing will vary.

Now, trace the word **white**.

white

Page 29

GRAY

Color the pictures **gray**.

Page 30

Draw something else that is **gray**.

Drawing will vary.

Now, trace the word **gray**.

gray

Page 31

Colors

Circle the **red** picture in each row.

Page 32

Colors

Circle the **yellow** picture in each row.

Page 33

Page 34

Page 35

Page 36

Page 37

Page 38

Page 39

Colors

Circle the **black** picture in each row.

Page 40

Colors

Circle the **white** picture in each row.

Page 41

Colors

Circle the **gray** picture in each row.

Page 42

Colors

In each row, color two things that are the same color.

Page 43

Colors

In each row, color two things that are the same color.

Page 44

Colors

In each row, color two things that are the same color.

Page 45

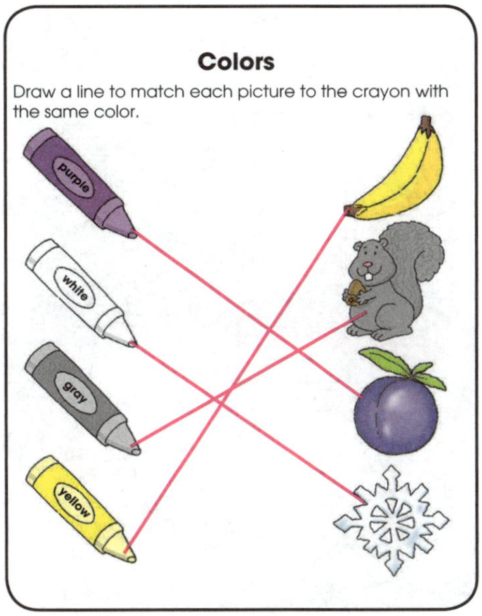

Page 46

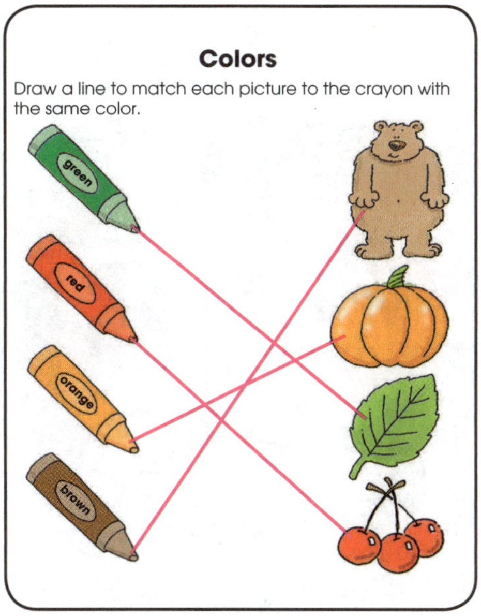

Page 47

Page 48

Page 49

Page 50

Page 51

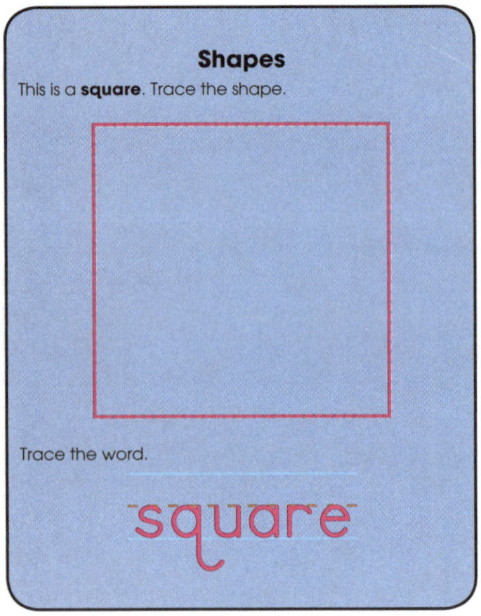

Page 52

Page 53

Page 54

Page 55

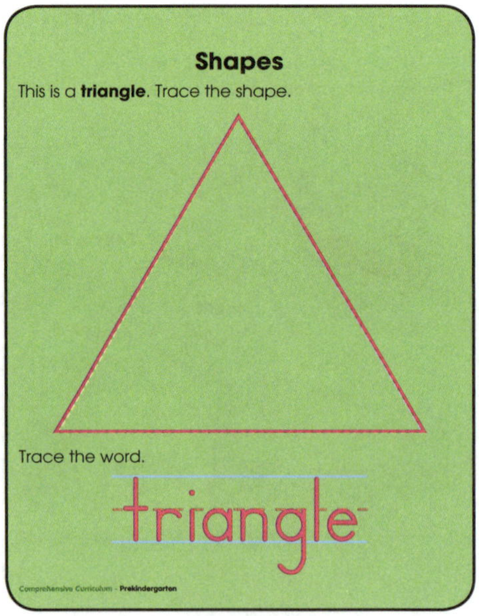

Page 56

Page 57

Shapes
This picture has **triangles** in it. Trace the triangles.

Page 58

Shapes
Color the **triangles**.

Page 59

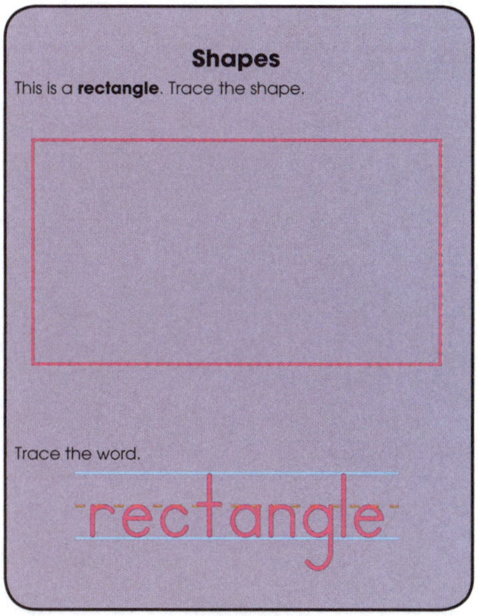
Shapes
This is a **rectangle**. Trace the shape.
Trace the word.
rectangle

Page 60

Shapes
This picture has **rectangles** in it. Trace the rectangles.

Page 61

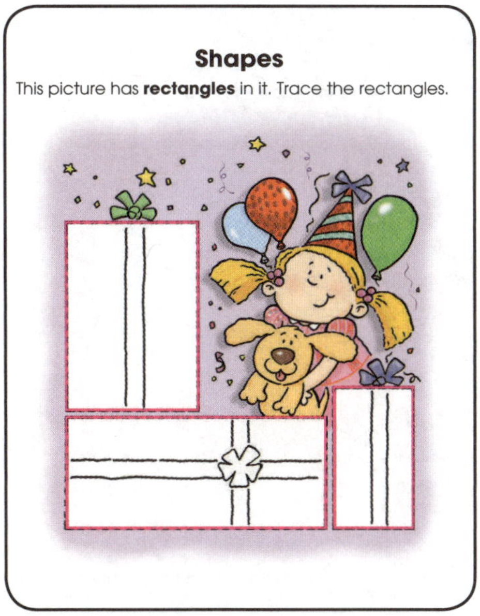
Shapes
This picture has **rectangles** in it. Trace the rectangles.

Page 62

Shapes
Color the **rectangles**.

Page 63

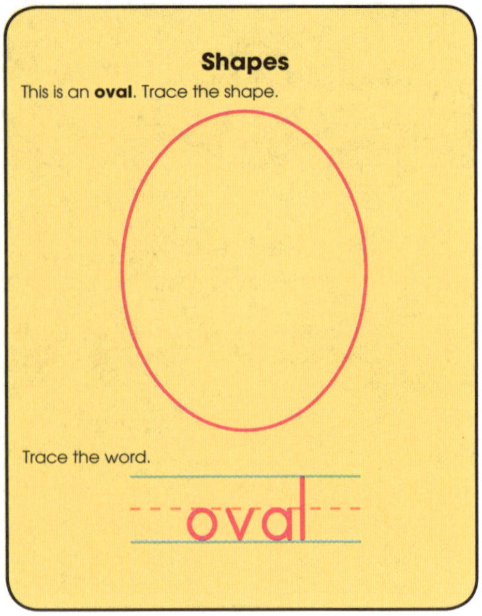

Page 64

Page 65

Page 66

Page 67

Page 68

Page 69

Page 70

Page 71

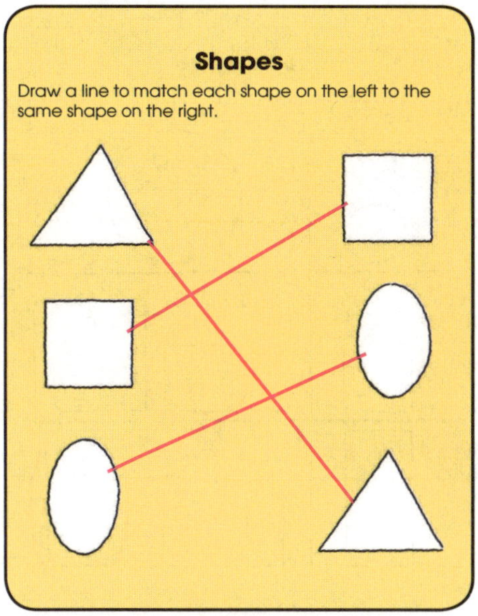

Page 72

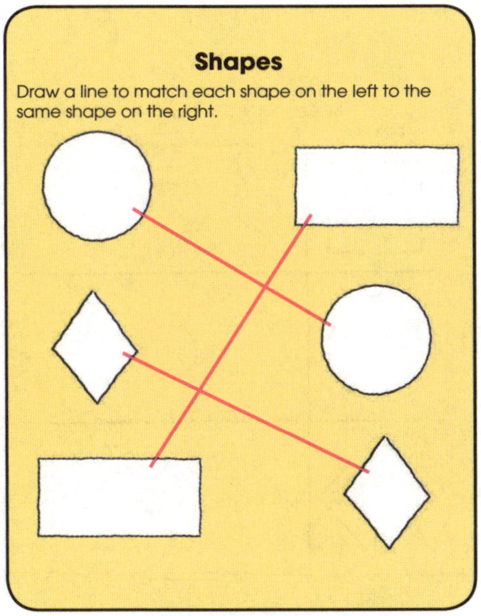

Page 73

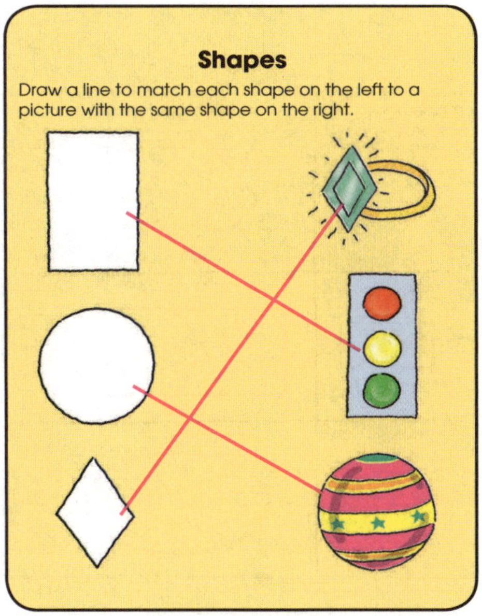

Page 74

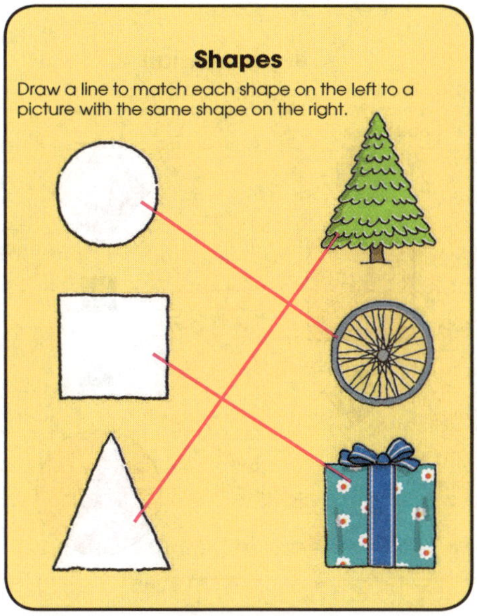

Page 75

Same Size

Circle the shape in each row that is the **same size** as the first shape.

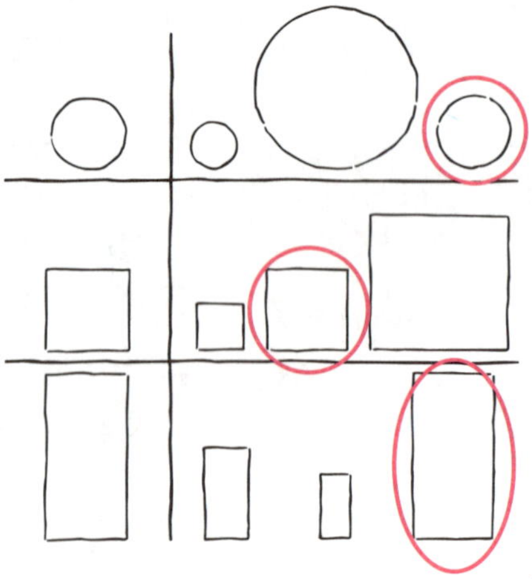

Page 76

Same Size

Circle the shape in each row that is the **same size** as the first shape.

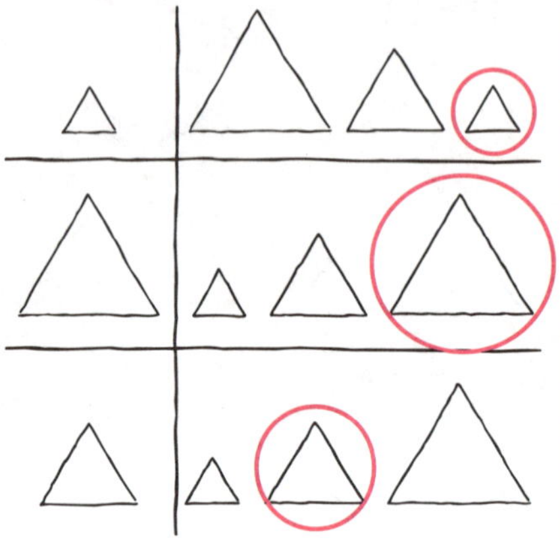

Page 77

Big and Small

Color the **big** shape in each box. Draw a line under the **small** shape in each box.

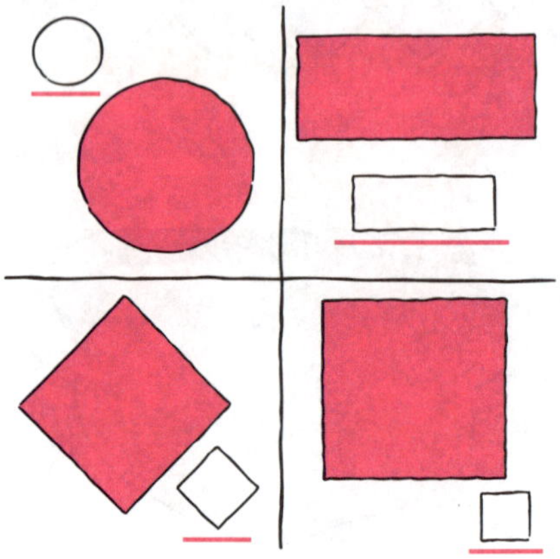

Page 78

Big and Small

Draw a line to match the shapes that are the same. Then, color each **big** shape red and each **small** shape green.

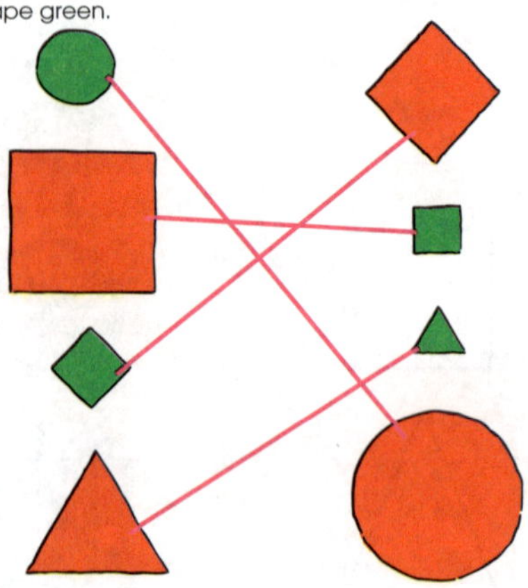

Page 79

Bigger

Name the shape in the box. Then, draw the same shape again. Make your shape **bigger** than the one in the box.

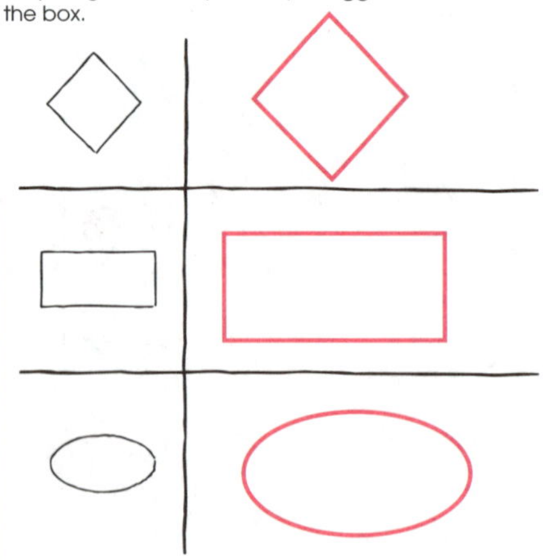

Page 80

Smaller

Name the shape in the box. Then, draw the same shape again. Make your shape **smaller** than the one in the box.

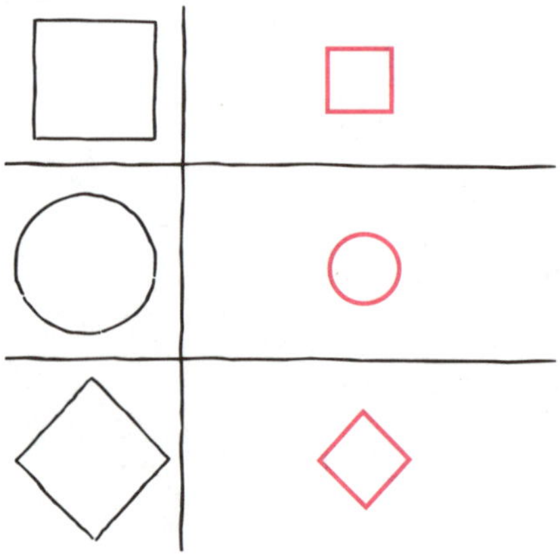

Page 81

Biggest
Find the **biggest** shape in each row. Color it orange.

Page 82

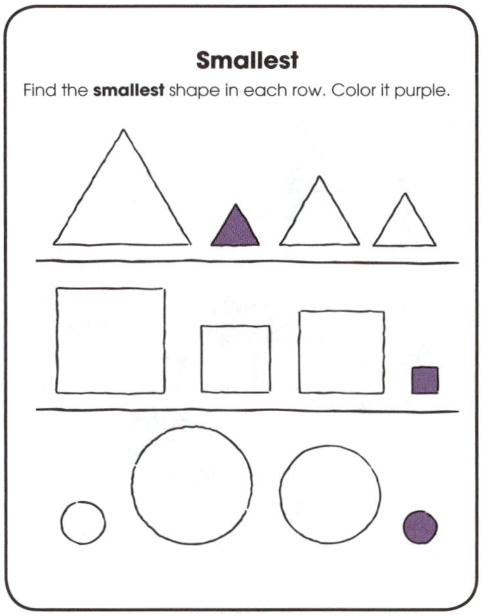
Smallest
Find the **smallest** shape in each row. Color it purple.

Page 83

Short and Tall
Circle each **short** person below. Draw a line under each **tall** person.

Page 84

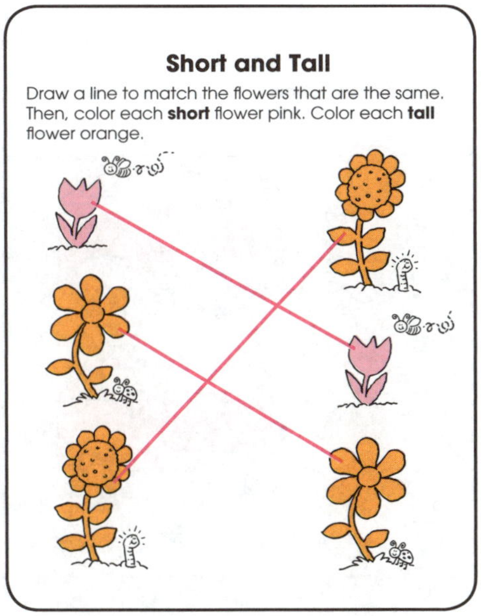
Short and Tall
Draw a line to match the flowers that are the same. Then, color each **short** flower pink. Color each **tall** flower orange.

Page 85

Shorter
Look at the glass below. Draw another glass beside it. Make your glass **shorter** than the first one.

Page 86

Taller
Look at the table below. Draw another table beside it. Make your table **taller** than the first one.

Page 87

Page 88

Page 89

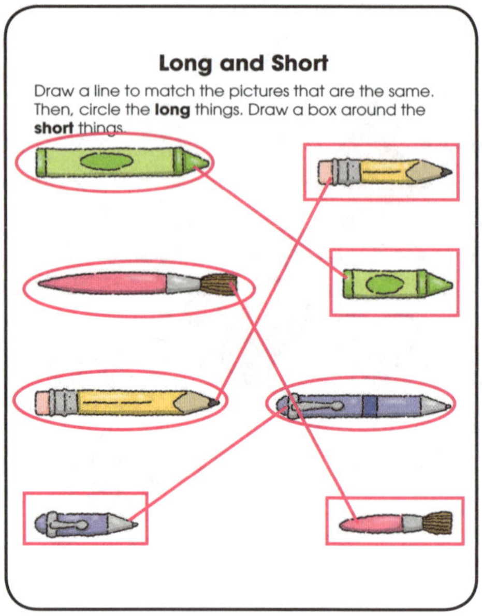

Page 90

Page 91

Page 92

Page 93

Longest

Name the animals in each row. Then, circle the animal with the **longest** tail.

Page 94

Shortest

Name the animals in each row. Then, circle the animal with the **shortest** tail.

Page 95

Size Review

Color the **longest** crayon red. Color the **shortest** crayon purple.

Circle the two bears that are the **same size**.

Page 96

Size Review

Color the **biggest** ball blue. Color the **smallest** ball green.

Draw a line under the **shortest** tree. Circle the **tallest** tree.

Page 97

Opposites

Look at the picture. Trace the word.

big

Page 98

Opposites

Look at the picture. Trace the word.

little

Page 99

Page 100

Page 101

Page 102

Page 103

Page 104

Page 105

Page 106

Page 107

Page 108

Page 109

Page 110

Page 111

Page 112

Page 113

Page 114

Page 115

Page 116

Page 117

Page 118

Page 119

Page 120

Page 121

Page 122

Page 123

Opposites

Look at the picture. Trace the word.

above

Page 124

Opposites

Look at the picture. Trace the word.

below

Page 125

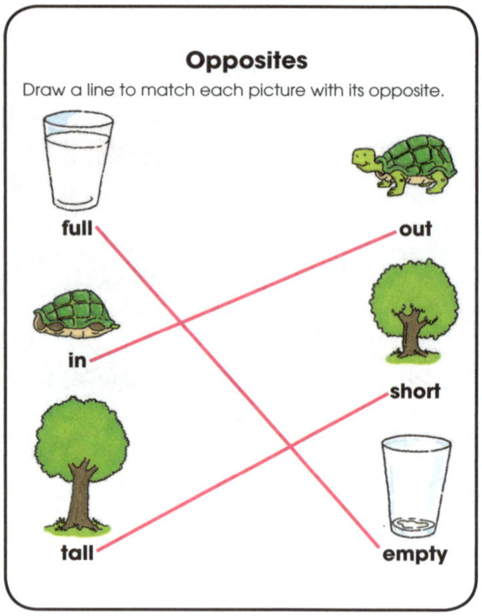
Opposites

Draw a line to match each picture with its opposite.

full, out, in, short, tall, empty

Page 126

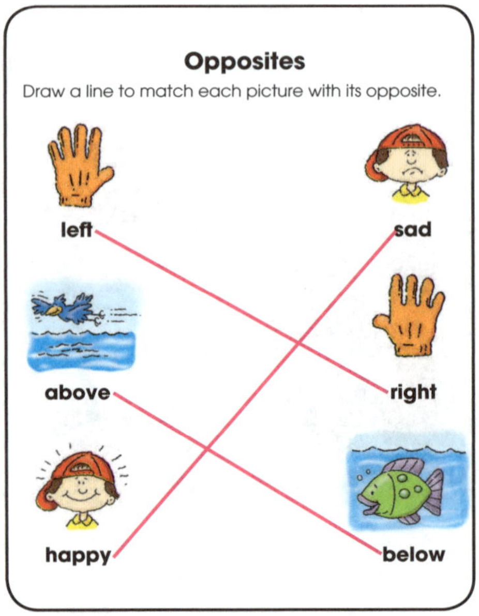
Opposites

Draw a line to match each picture with its opposite.

left, sad, above, right, happy, below

Page 127

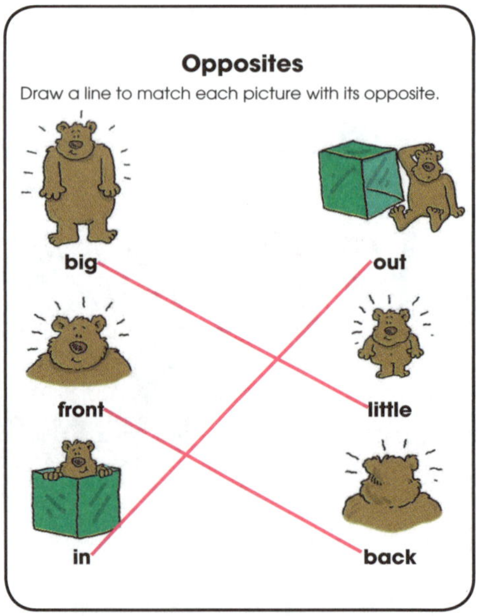
Opposites

Draw a line to match each picture with its opposite.

big, out, front, little, in, back

Page 128

Opposites

Look at the pictures in each row. Circle the picture that is the opposite of the first picture in each row.

Page 129

Opposites

Look at the pictures in each row. Circle the picture that is the opposite of the first picture in each row.

Page 130

Opposites

Cut out the pictures at the bottom of the page. Glue them in the correct places.

- Put the brown bear **inside** the house.
- Put the gray bear **outside** the house.
- Put the red bird **up** in the tree.
- Put the yellow bird **down** on the ground.

Page 131

Go-Togethers

Look at the pictures in each row. Circle the picture that goes together with the first picture.

Page 139

Go-Togethers

Look at the pictures in each row. Circle the picture that goes together with the first picture.

Page 140

Go-Togethers

Look at the pictures in each row. Cross out the picture that does not belong with the others.

Page 141

Go-Togethers

Look at the pictures in each row. Cross out the picture that does not belong with the others.

Page 142

Page 143

Page 144

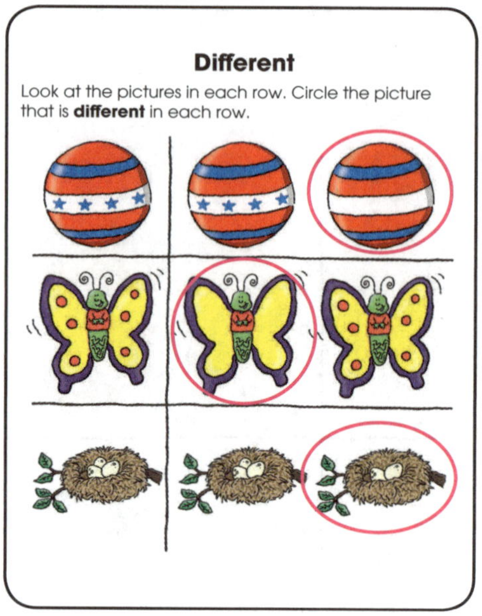

Page 145

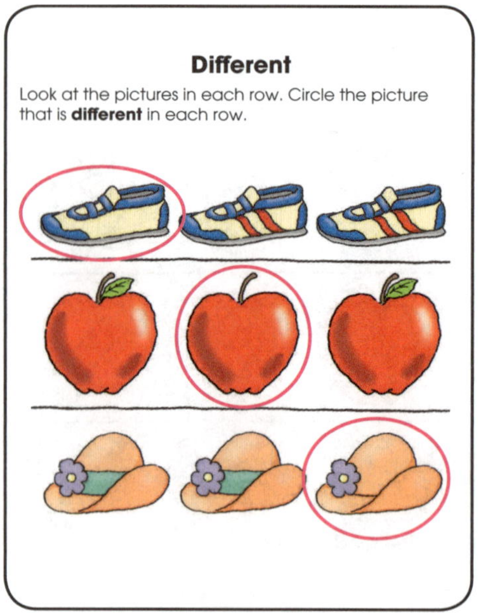

Page 146

Page 149

Page 150

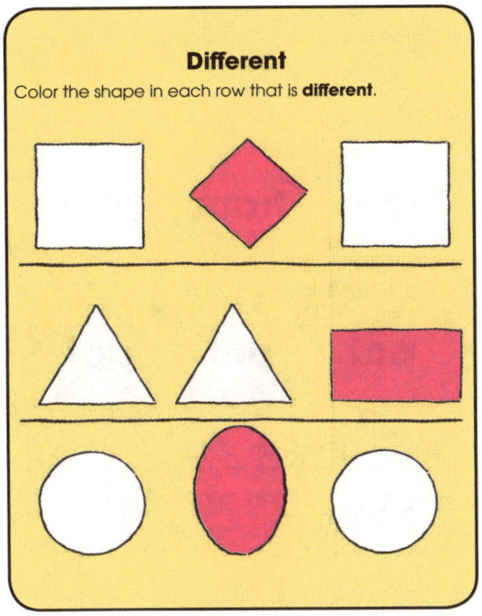
Different

Color the shape in each row that is **different**.

Page 151

Different

Color the shape in each row that is **different**.

Page 152

Same

Look at the letters in each row. Circle the letter that is the **same** as the first letter in each row.

Page 153

Same

Look at the letters in each row. Circle the letter that is the **same** as the first letter in each row.

Page 154

Same

Look at the letters in each row. Circle the letter that is the **same** as the first letter in each row.

Page 155

Same

Look at the letters in each row. Circle the letter that is the **same** as the first letter in each row.

Page 156

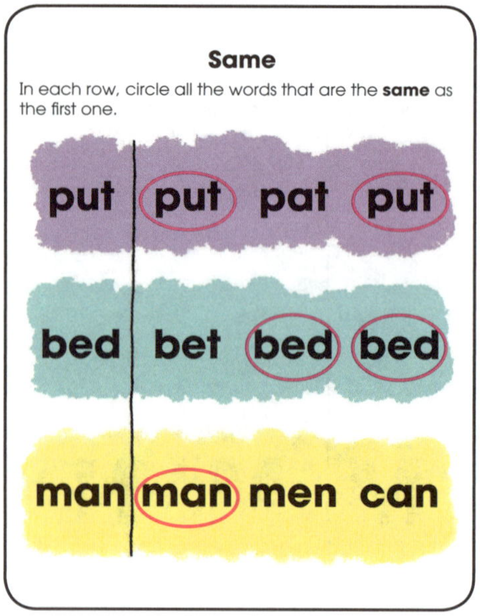

Same

In each row, circle all the words that are the **same** as the first one.

put | put pat put

bed | bet bed bed

man | man men can

Page 159

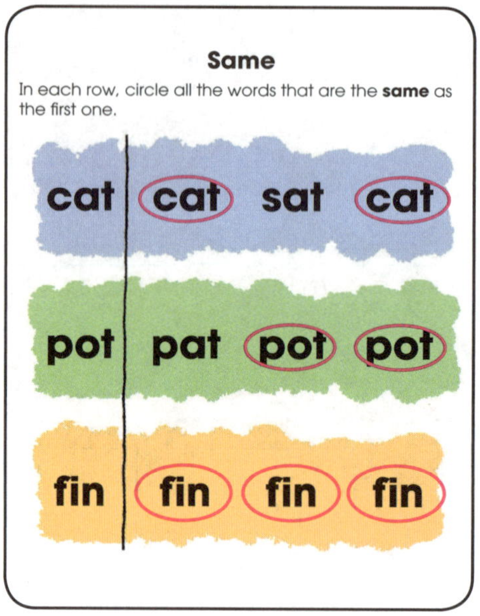

Same

In each row, circle all the words that are the **same** as the first one.

cat | cat sat cat

pot | pat pot pot

fin | fin fin fin

Page 160

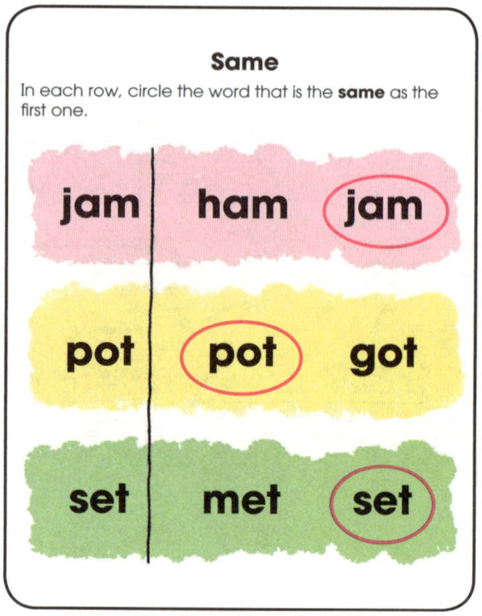

Same

In each row, circle the word that is the **same** as the first one.

jam | ham jam

pot | pot got

set | met set

Page 161

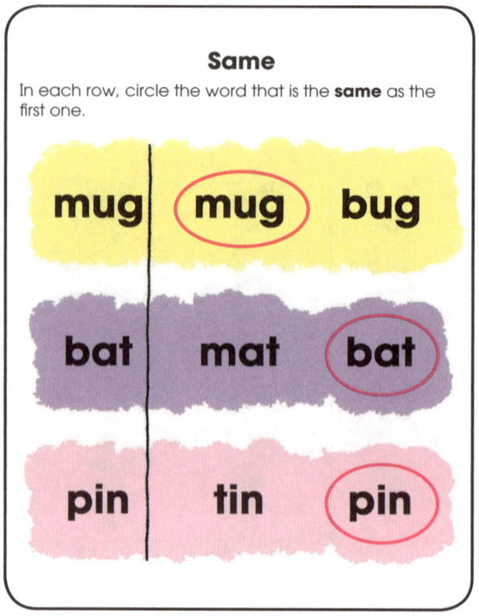

Same

In each row, circle the word that is the **same** as the first one.

mug | mug bug

bat | mat bat

pin | tin pin

Page 162

Left to Right

Help the cat get to the milk. Follow the arrow to trace a path to the milk.

Help the rabbit get to the carrot. Follow the arrow to trace a path to the carrot.

Page 164

Left to Right

Help the bear get to the honey. Follow the arrow to trace a path to the honey.

Help the cow get to the grass. Follow the arrow to trace a path to the grass.

Page 165

Page 166

Page 167

Page 168

Page 169

Page 170

Page 171

Page 172

Page 173

Page 174

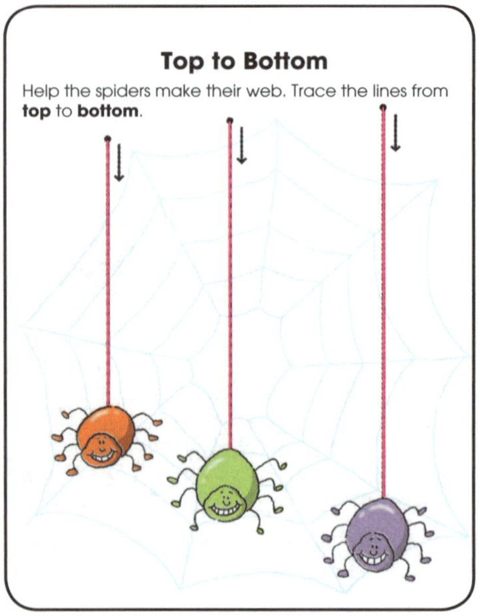

Page 175

Page 176

Page 177

Page 178

Page 179

Page 180

Page 181

Page 182

Page 183

Page 184

Page 185

Page 186

Page 187

Page 188

Page 189

Slanted Lines

Start at the top. Follow the arrows to trace the dotted lines.

Page 190

Curved Lines

Start at the dots on the left. Follow the arrows to trace the dotted lines.

Page 191

Curved Lines

Start at the dots on the right. Follow the arrows to trace the dotted lines.

Page 192

Ovals

Start at the dots. Follow the arrows to trace the dotted lines.

Page 193

Ovals

Start at the dots. Follow the arrows to trace the dotted lines.

Page 194

A

Trace UPPERCASE **A**.

Now, write UPPERCASE **A**.

Page 196

Page 197

Page 198

Page 199

Page 201

Page 202

Page 203

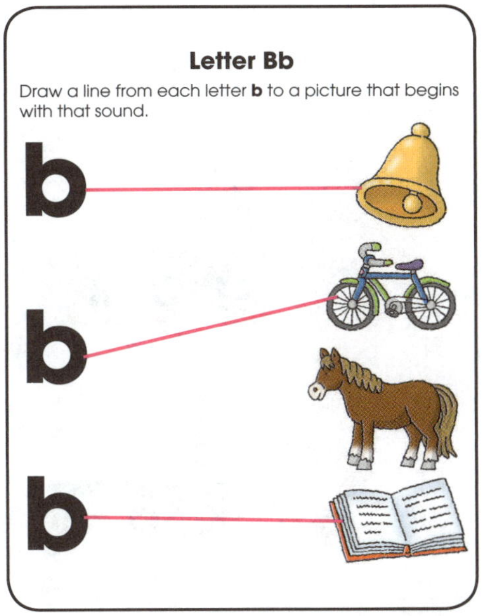

Page 204

Page 205

Page 206

Page 207

Page 208

Page 209

Letter Cc

Look at the patterns on the cats' sweaters. Draw a line between the cats with matching **Cc** patterns on their sweaters.

Page 211

Letter Review

Look at the letter each person is holding. Circle the same letter in each box.

Page 212

Letter Review

Look at the letter each person is holding. Circle the same letter in each box.

Page 213

Trace UPPERCASE **D**.

Now, write UPPERCASE **D**.

Page 214

Trace lowercase **d**.

Now, write lowercase **d**.

Page 215

Letter Dd

Say the names of the pictures. Color each picture that begins with the sound of **Dd**.

Page 216

Page 217

Page 218

Page 219

Page 220

Page 221

Page 222

Letter Review

Trace the letters on the caterpillar. Write the missing letters where they belong.

Page 223

Trace UPPERCASE **F**.

Now, write UPPERCASE **F**.

Page 224

Trace lowercase **f**.

Now, write lowercase **f**.

Page 225

Letter Ff

Say the names of the pictures. Color each picture that begins with the sound of **Ff**.

Page 226

Letter Ff

Say the names of the pictures on the frogs. Cut out each frog that has a picture that begins with the sound of **Ff**. Then, glue the **Ff** frogs on the lily pads.

Page 227

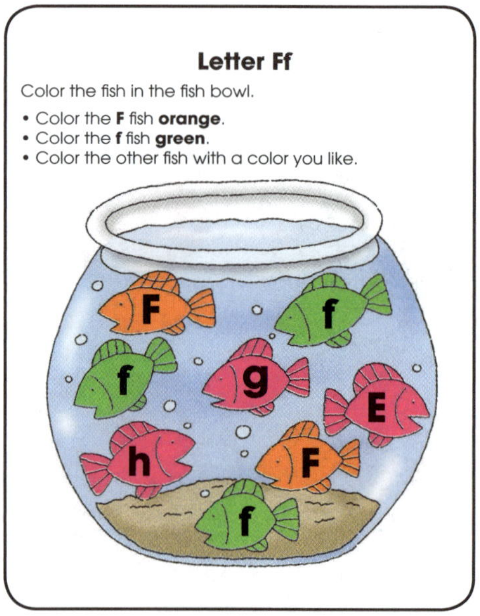
Letter Ff

Color the fish in the fish bowl.

- Color the **F** fish **orange**.
- Color the **f** fish **green**.
- Color the other fish with a color you like.

Page 229

Page 230

Page 231

Page 232

Page 233

Page 234

Page 235

Page 236

Page 237

Page 238

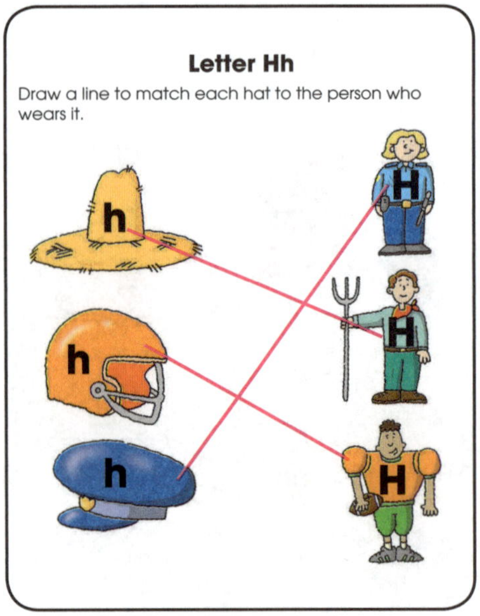

Page 239

Page 240

Page 241

Page 242

Page 243

Page 244

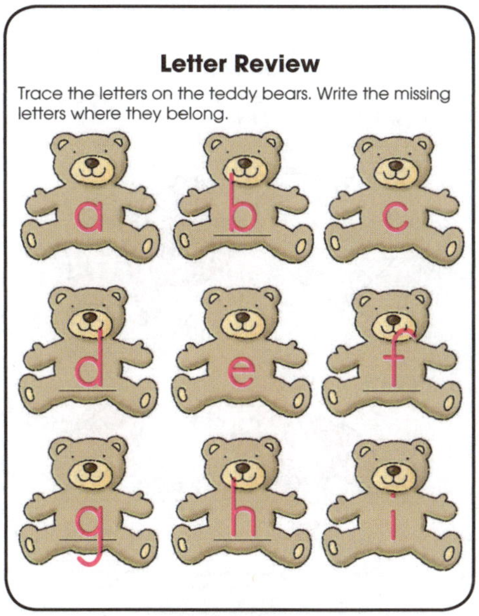

Page 245

Page 246

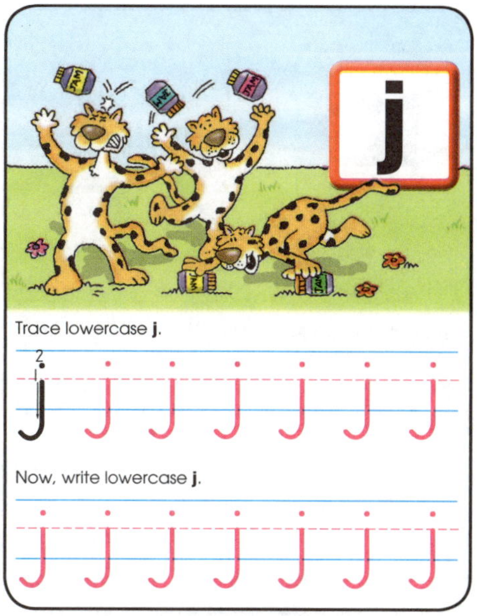

Page 247

Letter Jj

Say the names of the pictures. Color each picture that begins with the sound of **Jj**.

Page 248

Letter Jj

Help the juggler. Cut out the balls that begin with the sound of **Jj**. Glue them on the balls the juggler is juggling.

Page 249

Letter Jj

Jim has a ticket for a ride. Color to find the hidden picture.

- Color the spaces with **J** or **j** **blue**.
- Color the other spaces **gray**.

What will Jim ride in? A jet

Page 251

Trace UPPERCASE **K**.

Now, write UPPERCASE **K**.

Page 252

Trace lowercase **k**.

Now, write lowercase **k**.

Page 253

Letter Kk

Say the names of the pictures. Color each picture that begins with the sound of **Kk**.

Page 254

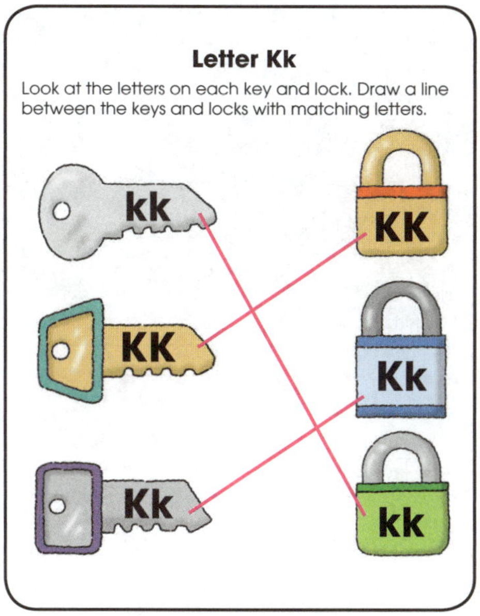
Letter Kk

Look at the letters on each key and lock. Draw a line between the keys and locks with matching letters.

Page 255

Letter Kk

Say the names of the pictures on the kites. If a picture begins with the **Kk** sound, draw a kite string from the kite to a child's hand.

Page 256

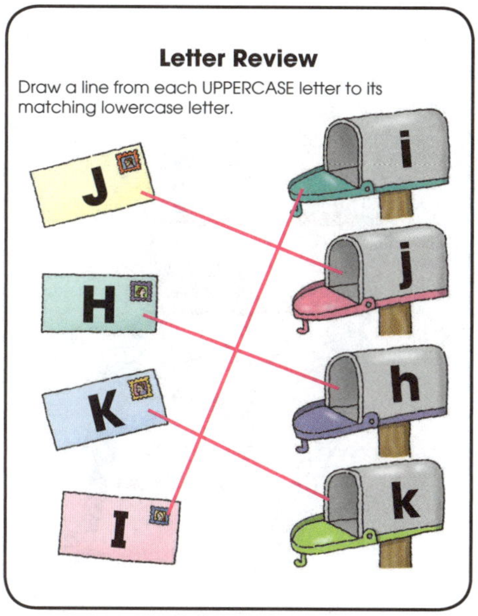
Letter Review

Draw a line from each UPPERCASE letter to its matching lowercase letter.

Page 257

Trace UPPERCASE **L**.

Now, write UPPERCASE **L**.

Page 258

Trace lowercase **l**.

Now, write lowercase **l**.

Page 259

Letter Ll

Say the names of the pictures. Color each picture that begins with the sound of **Ll**.

Page 260

Letter Ll

Climb the ladder by coloring the pictures that begin with the sound of **Ll**.

Page 261

Trace UPPERCASE **M**.

Now, write UPPERCASE **M**.

Page 262

Trace lowercase **m**.

Now, write lowercase **m**.

Page 263

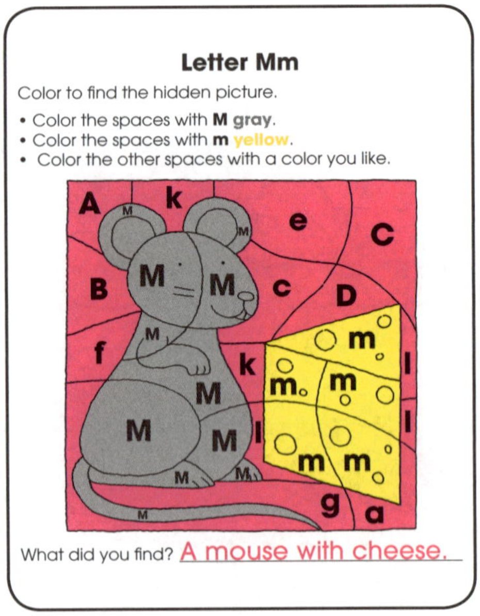
Letter Mm

Color to find the hidden picture.

- Color the spaces with **M** **gray**.
- Color the spaces with **m** **yellow**.
- Color the other spaces with a color you like.

What did you find? A mouse with cheese.

Page 264

Letter Mm

Help the mouse get to the cheese. Say the name of each picture. Follow the path of pictures that begin with the sound of **Mm**.

Page 265

Trace UPPERCASE **N**.

Now, write UPPERCASE **N**.

Page 266

Page 267

Page 268

Page 269

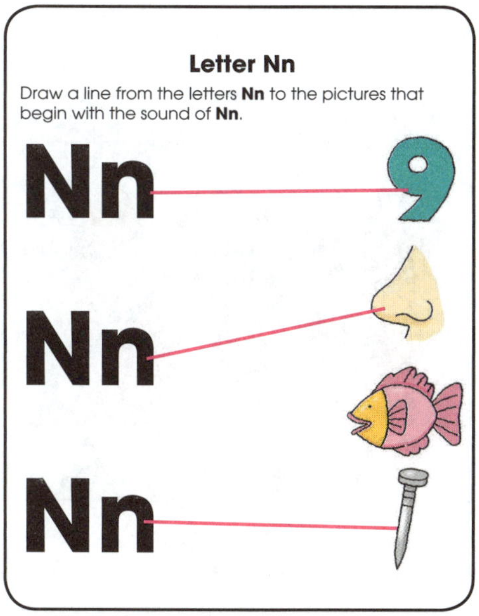

Page 271

Page 272

Page 273

Letter Oo

Say the names of the pictures. Color each picture that begins with the sound of **Oo**.

Page 274

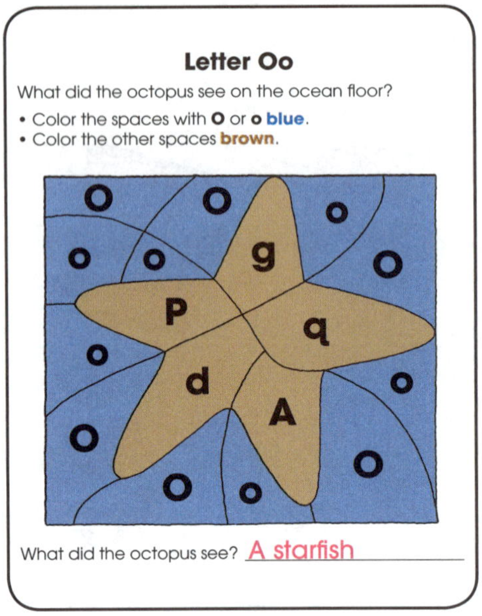

Letter Oo

What did the octopus see on the ocean floor?

- Color the spaces with **O** or **o** **blue**.
- Color the other spaces **brown**.

What did the octopus see? A starfish

Page 275

Trace UPPERCASE **P**.

Now, write UPPERCASE **P**.

Page 276

Trace lowercase **p**.

Now, write lowercase **p**.

Page 277

Letter Pp

Say the names of the pictures. Color each picture that begins with the sound of **Pp**.

Page 278

Letter Pp

Cut out the party hats with **P** or **p**. Glue them on the children's heads.

Page 279

Page 285

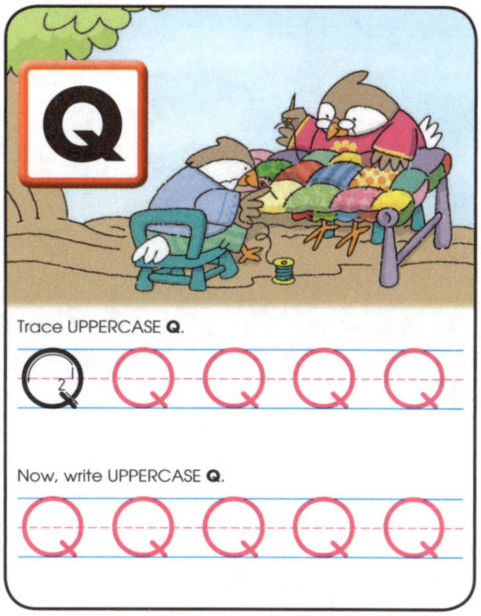

Page 286

Page 287

Page 288

Page 289

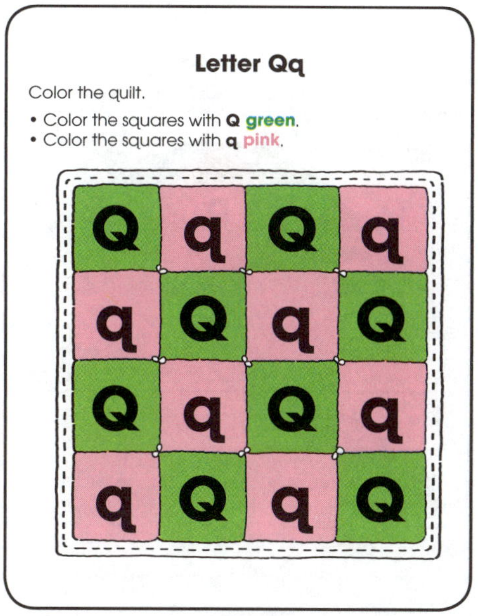

Page 291

Page 292

Page 293

Page 294

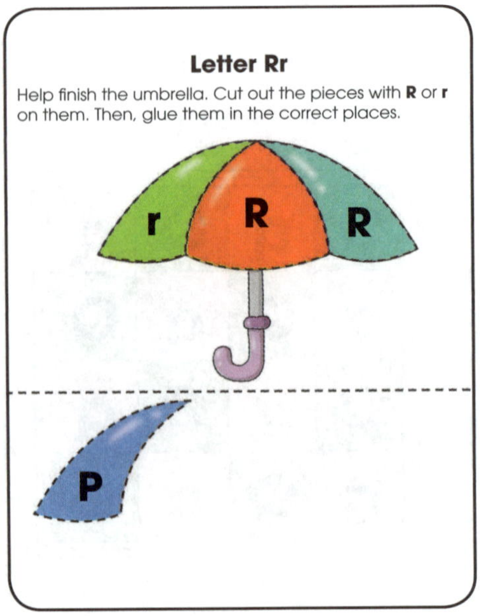

Page 295

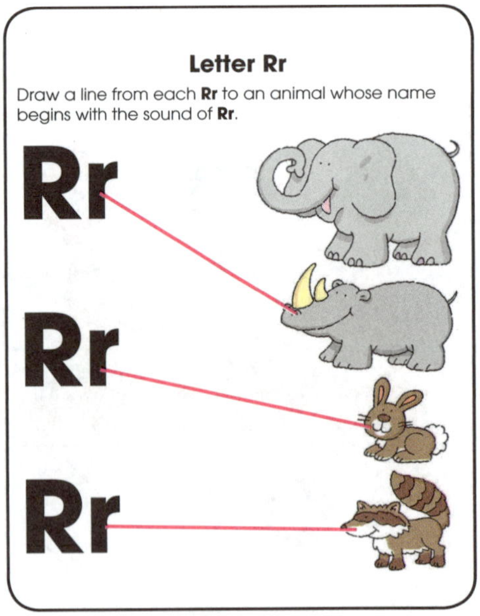

Page 297

Page 298

S

Trace lowercase **s**.

s s s s s s s

Now, write lowercase **s**.

s s s s s s s

Page 299

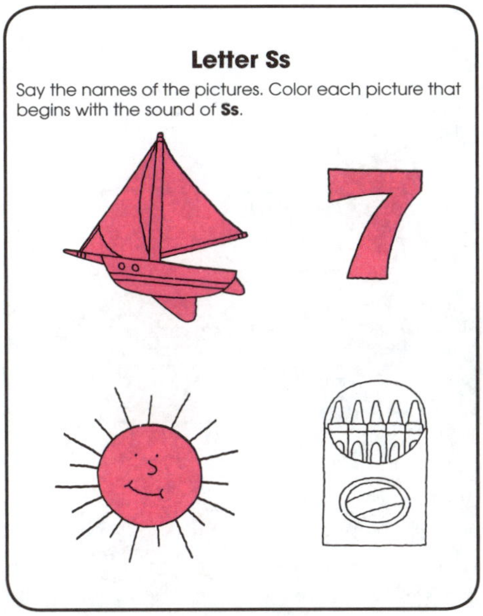
Letter Ss

Say the names of the pictures. Color each picture that begins with the sound of **Ss**.

Page 300

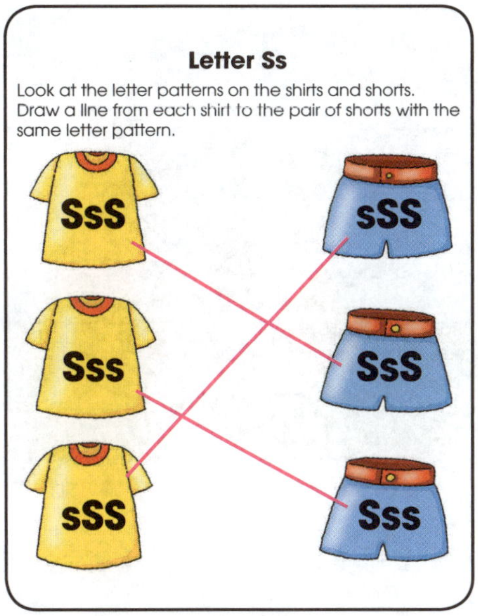
Letter Ss

Look at the letter patterns on the shirts and shorts. Draw a line from each shirt to the pair of shorts with the same letter pattern.

Page 301

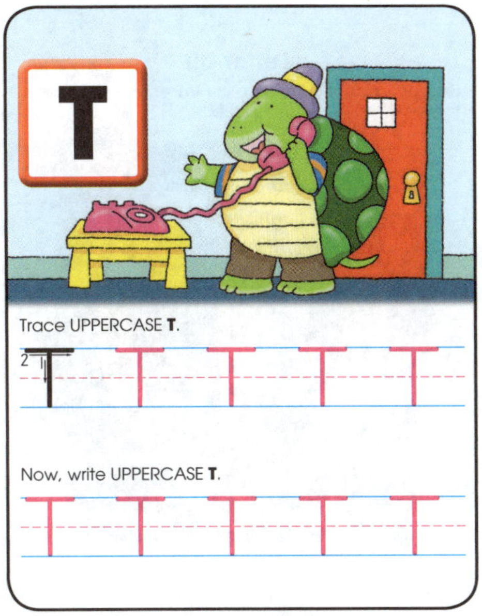
T

Trace UPPERCASE **T**.

T T T T T

Now, write UPPERCASE **T**.

T T T T T

Page 302

t

Trace lowercase **t**.

t t t t t t t

Now, write lowercase **t**.

t t t t t t t

Page 303

Letter Tt

Say the names of the pictures. Color each picture that begins with the sound of **Tt**.

Page 304

Page 305

Page 307

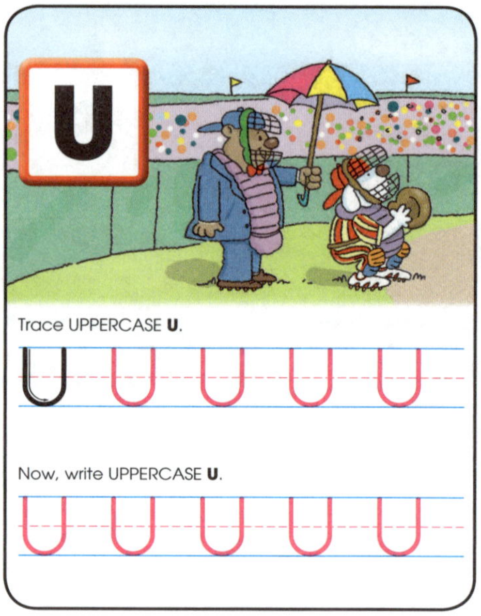

Page 308

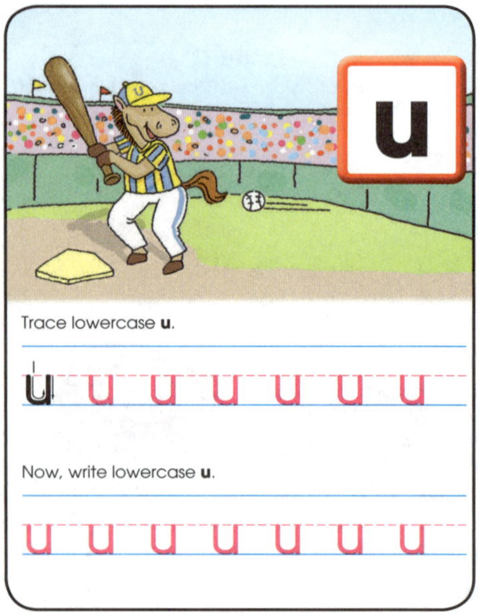

Page 309

Page 310

Page 311

Page 312

Page 313

Page 314

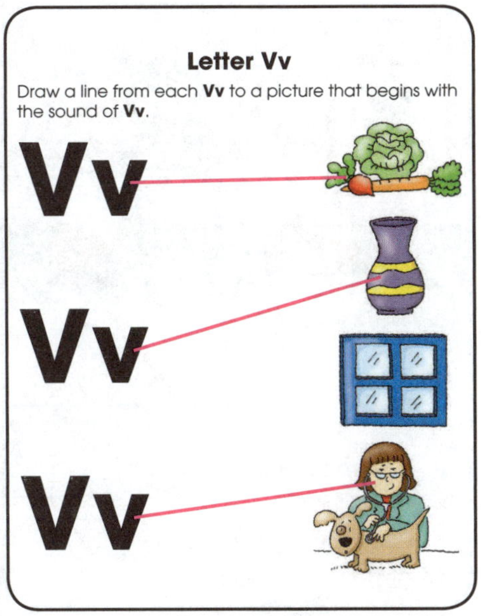

Page 315

Page 316

Page 317

Page 318

Page 319

Page 321

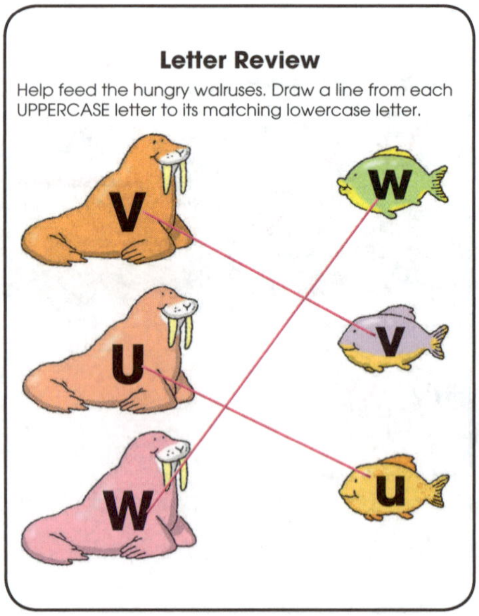

Page 322

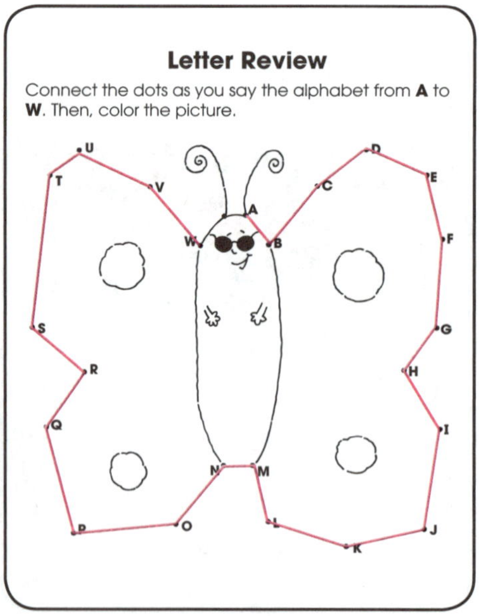

Page 323

Page 324

Trace lowercase **x**.

Now, write lowercase **x**.

Page 325

Letter Xx

Say the names of the pictures. Color each picture that begins with the sound of **Xx**.

Page 326

Letter Xx

Say the names of the pictures below. Then, trace the **x** to complete each word.

Page 327

Trace UPPERCASE **Y**.

Now, write UPPERCASE **Y**.

Page 328

Trace lowercase **y**.

Now, write lowercase **y**.

Page 329

Letter Yy

Say the names of the pictures. Color each picture that begins with the sound of **Yy**.

Page 330

Letter Yy

Color to find the hidden picture.

- Color the spaces with **Y** yellow.
- Color the other spaces orange.

What did you find? the letter Y

Page 331

Trace UPPERCASE **Z**.

Z Z Z Z Z

Now, write UPPERCASE **Z**.

Z Z Z Z Z

Page 332

Trace lowercase **z**.

z z z z z z z

Now, write lowercase **z**.

z z z z z z z

Page 333

Letter Zz

Say the names of the pictures. Color each picture that begins with the sound of **Zz**.

Page 334

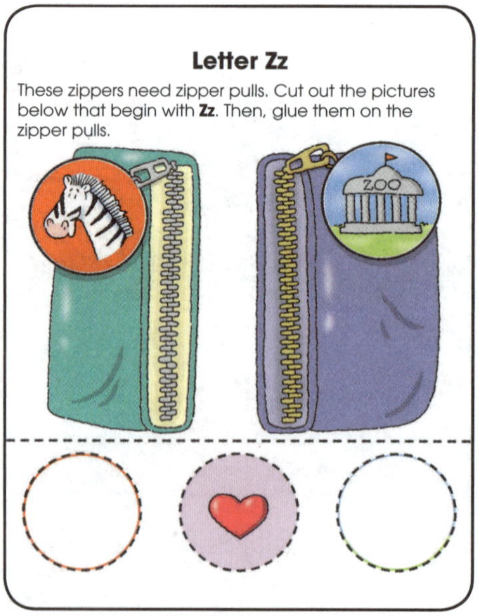

Letter Zz

These zippers need zipper pulls. Cut out the pictures below that begin with **Zz**. Then, glue them on the zipper pulls.

Page 335

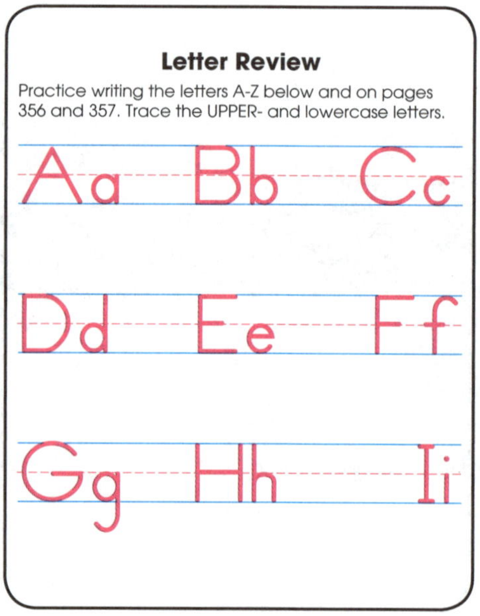

Letter Review

Practice writing the letters A-Z below and on pages 356 and 357. Trace the UPPER- and lowercase letters.

Aa Bb Cc

Dd Ee Ff

Gg Hh Ii

Page 355

Letter Review

Jj Kk Ll

Mm Nn Oo

Pp Qq Rr

Page 356

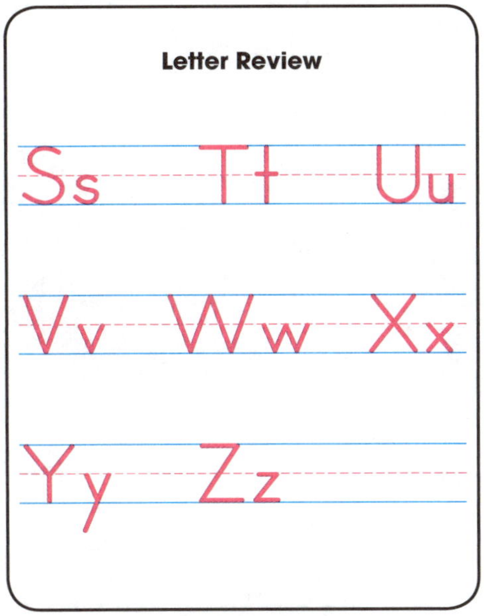
Letter Review

Ss Tt Uu

Vv Ww Xx

Yy Zz

Page 357

Beginning Sounds

Look at the pictures in each row. Circle the sound each picture begins with. Then, color the pictures.

s n p d g b

t r l h s m

Page 358

Beginning Sounds

Look at the pictures in each row. Color the picture that has the same beginning sound as the first picture.

Page 359

Beginning Sounds

Look at the pictures in each row. Color two pictures in each row that begin with the same sound.

Page 360

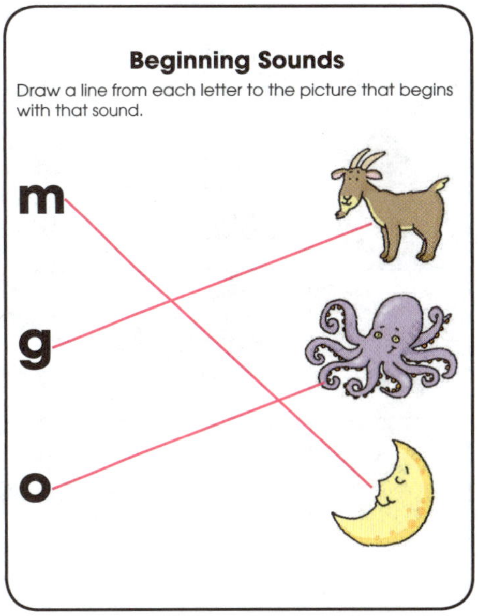
Beginning Sounds

Draw a line from each letter to the picture that begins with that sound.

m

g

o

Page 361

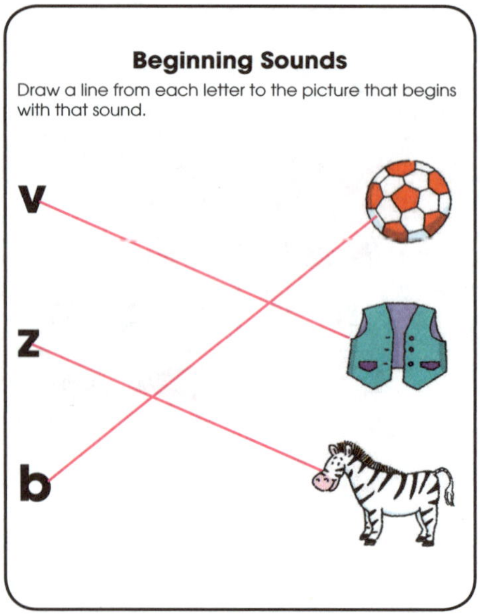

Page 362

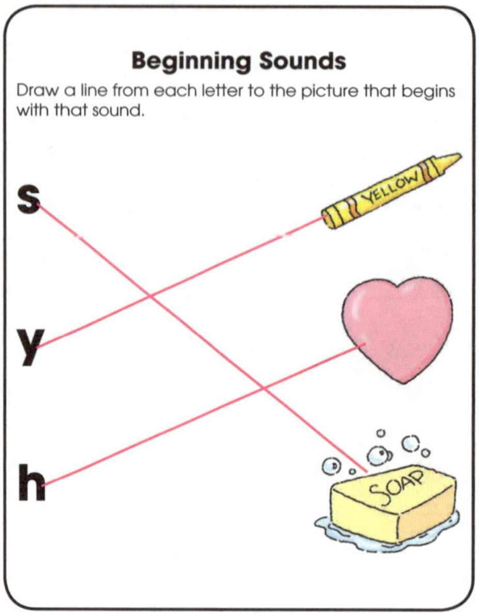

Page 363

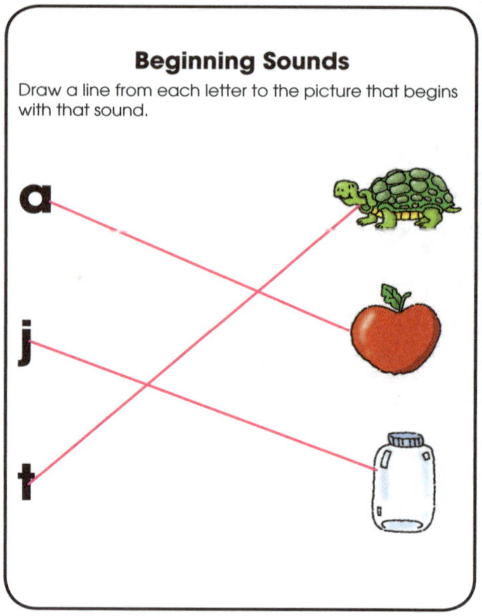

Page 364

Page 365

Page 366

Page 367

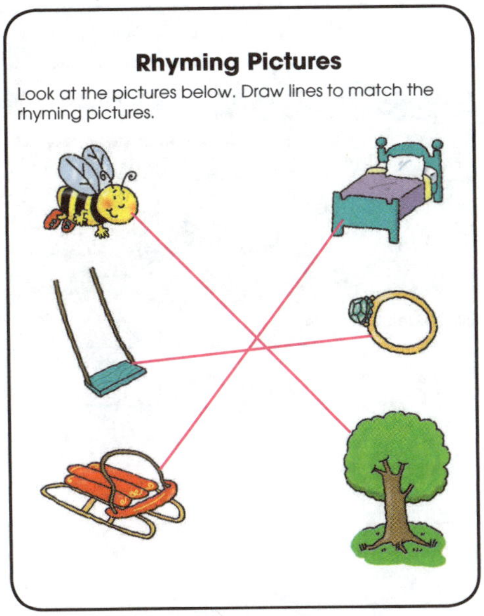

Page 368

Page 369

Page 370

Page 372

Page 373

Page 374

Page 375

Page 376

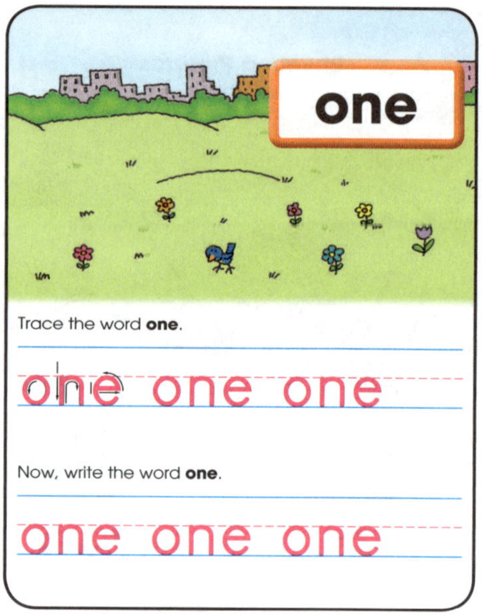

Page 377

Page 378

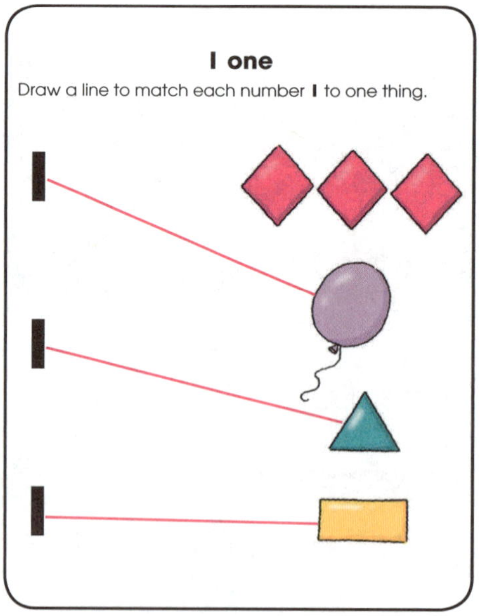

Page 379

Page 380

two

Trace the word **two**.

two two two

Now, write the word **two**.

two two two

Page 381

2 two

Draw a line to match each number **2** to a group of **2** things.

2

2

2

Page 382

2 two

Draw another picture in each box to make **2** of each thing.

Page 383

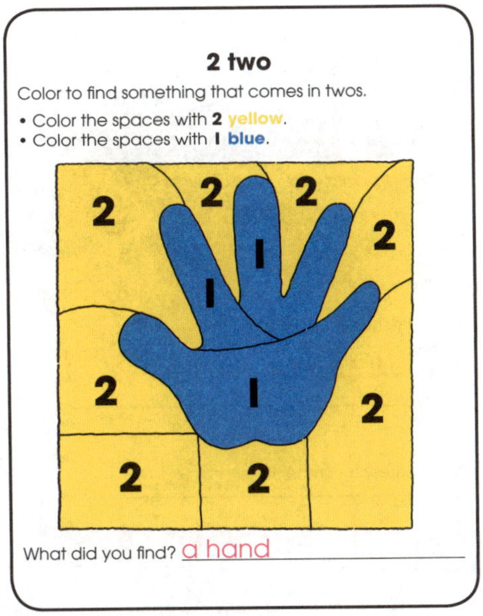

2 two

Color to find something that comes in twos.

- Color the spaces with **2** yellow.
- Color the spaces with **1** **blue**.

What did you find? a hand

Page 384

2 two

Circle **2** pictures in each box. Then, write the number **2** on the line in each box.

2 2 2 2

Page 385

3

Trace the number **3**.

3 3 3 3 3 3

Now, write the number **3**.

3 3 3 3 3 3

Page 386

Page 387

Page 388

Page 389

Page 390

Page 391

Page 392

Page 393

Page 394

Page 395

Page 396

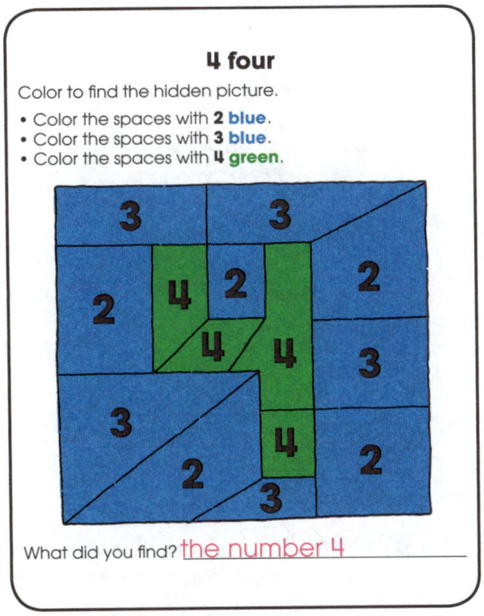

Page 397

Page 398

Page 399

Page 400

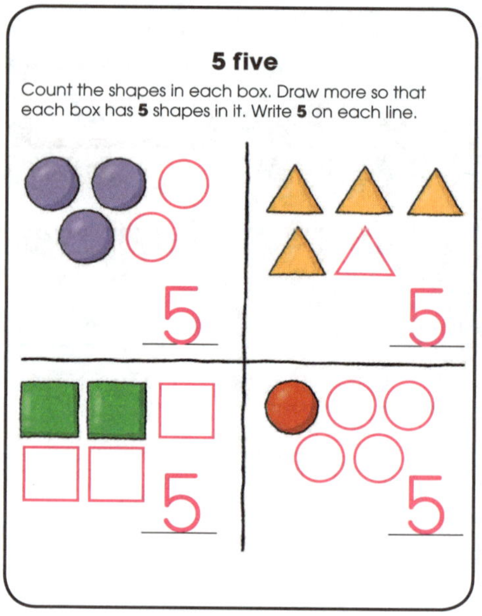

Page 401

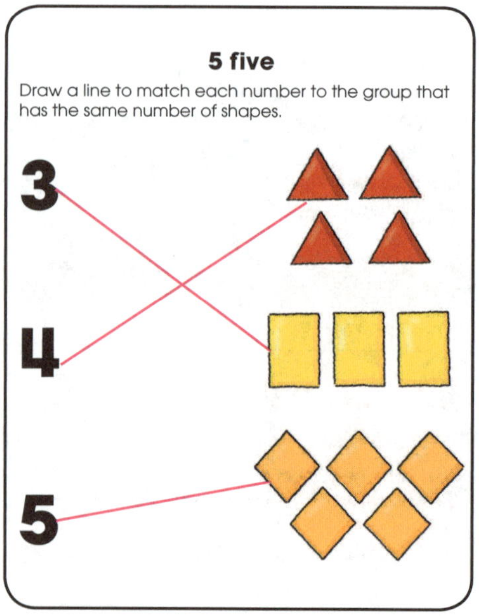

Page 402

Page 403

Page 404

Page 405

Page 406

Page 407

Page 408

Page 409

Page 410

Page 411

Page 412

Page 413

Page 414

Page 415

Page 416

Page 417

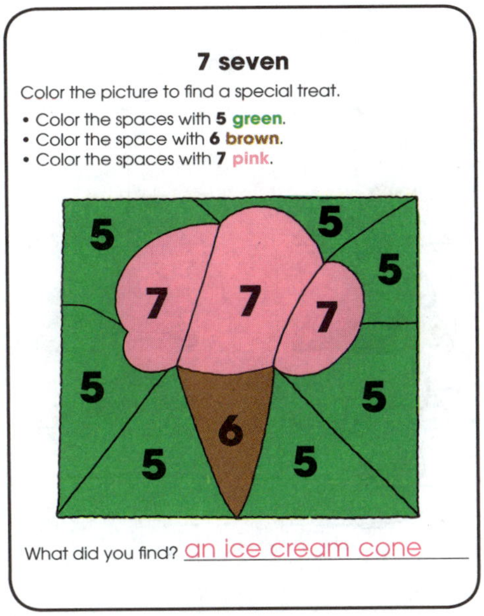

Page 418

Page 419

Page 420

Page 421

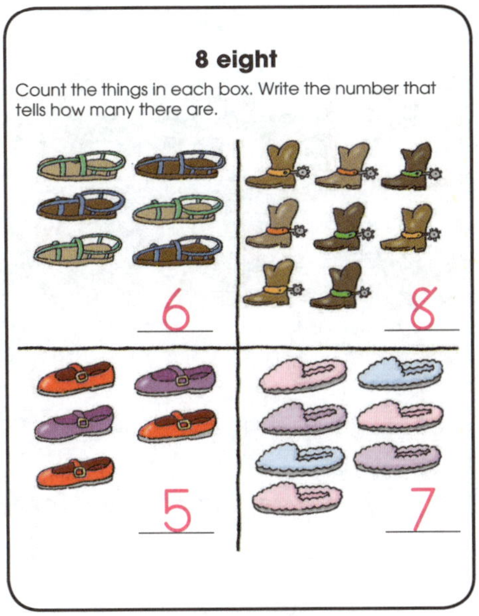

Page 422

Page 423

Page 424

Page 425

Page 426

Page 427

Page 428

Page 429

Page 430

Page 431

Page 432

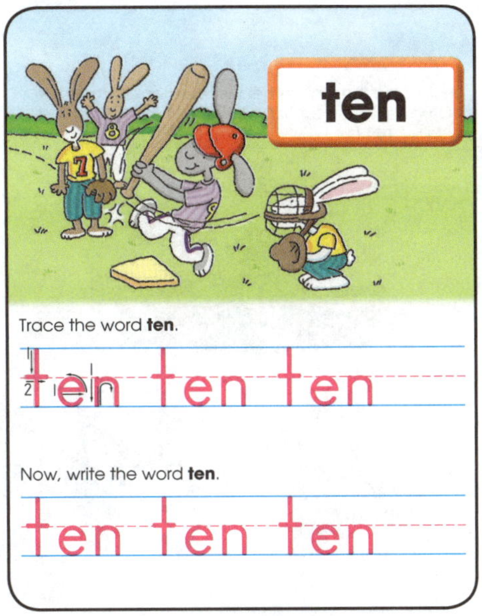

Page 433

Page 434

Page 435

Page 436

Page 437

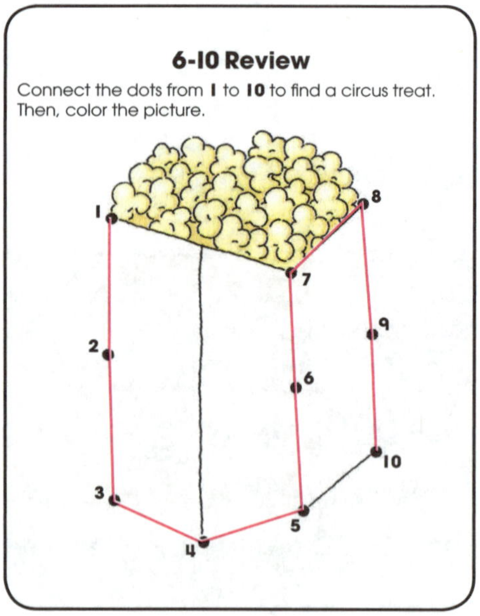

Page 438

Page 451

Page 452

Page 453

Page 454

Page 455

Page 456

Page 457

Page 458

ANSWER KEY

One-to-One Correspondence

Trace the string from the cat to the ball of yarn. Then, draw more balls of yarn so each cat has one to play with.

Page 459

More and Fewer

Count the blocks each child is playing with. Circle the child who has **more** blocks.

Page 460

More and Fewer

Count the blocks in each group. Circle the group of blocks that has **more**.

Page 461

More and Fewer

Count the blocks in the first box. Then, draw a group of blocks that has **more**.

Page 462

More and Fewer

Count the cars each child is playing with. Circle the child who has **fewer** cars.

Page 463

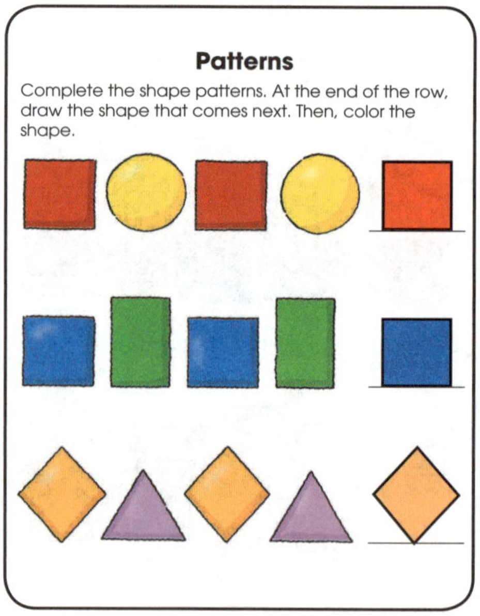
Patterns

Complete the shape patterns. At the end of the row, draw the shape that comes next. Then, color the shape.

Page 464

Patterns

Complete the picture patterns. At the end of the row, draw the picture that comes next.

Page 465

Patterns

Complete the picture patterns. Draw what is missing on the last picture in each row.

Page 466

Patterns

Complete the letter patterns. At the end of the row, write the letter that comes next.

C O C O C O

B P B P B P

M N M N M N

Page 467

Patterns

Complete the letter patterns. At the end of the row, write the letter that comes next.

L L H L L H

V V X V V X

B B D B B D

Page 468

Name ____________________

Aa Bb Cc

Dd Ee Ff

Gg Hh Ii

Jj Kk Ll

Mm Nn Oo

Pp Qq Rr

Name ______________________

Ss Tt Uu

Vv Ww

Xx Yy Zz

The teaching suggestions on the following pages are a springboard for further learning. Use these activities to spend important time talking and interacting with your child on a daily basis.

Basic Concepts/Skills

- Use color/shape/size words daily when speaking to your child. "The grass is GREEN." "This plate is a CIRCLE." "See the BIG dog."
- Take a color or shape walk with your child. Before you begin, let your child choose between two colors or shapes. Take an object of that color or shape with you on your walk. Ask your child to look for objects that are the same color or shape as the object he chose.
- Help your child learn colors, shapes, and sizes by making up poems or songs to recite or sing every day.
- From construction paper, cut shapes (squares, ovals, circles, rectangles, triangles, diamonds) and sizes (small, medium, large) from several colors (red, green, blue, yellow, etc.). Have your child sort the shapes according to the category you name.
- Read color, shape, and size books with your child. Try the following books by Tana Hoban: *Shapes, Shapes, Shapes; Colors Everywhere; Is It Larger? Is It Smaller?;* and *Is It Red? Is It Yellow? Is It Blue?* You might also read *Color* by Christina Rossetti or any version of *The Three Bears.*
- Use a craft knife to cut shape stencils from plastic lids. Have your child use the stencils to create shape pictures.
- Place two similar objects in front of your child. Talk to her about how they are the same. Then, place two objects that are not alike in front of your child. Talk to her about how they are different.

- Using poster board or heavy paper, cut 10 cards measuring 12" x 6". Draw a heavy line down the middle of each. Write two sets of letters, one on each side. Make some of the letter cards the same and some different. Turn the cards upside down, and have your child find the type of matches you specify—same or different—until all the cards are turned over.
- With your child, look through your pantry or cupboards for food containers that are the same and those that are different. Then, set out several pairs of containers, mix them up, and have your child match the correct pairs.
- Soak several pairs of cotton balls with different scents (perfumes, scented oils, spices, etc.). Mix up the pairs. Have your child match the scents that smell the same.

Reading Readiness

- Read books and a variety of other things (cereal boxes, food labels, cards, road signs, newspapers, magazines, etc.) with your child daily. Run your finger under the words as you read them, so your child learns that words have meaning and are read from left to right. Let your child see you reading. Take your child to the library, and let him choose one or two books to read, or sign him up for story hour.
- Show your child that you value books. Show him the proper way to hold a book, to store and put away a book, and to turn the pages. Let your child see you handling books with care.
- Read books to your child that contain lots of rhyme and repetition, such as *Mary Wore Her Red Dress* by Merle Peek; *I Went Walking* by Sue Williams; *Brown Bear, Brown Bear, What Do You See?* by Bill Martin, Jr; and *Millions of Cats* by Wanda Ga'g. The children's librarian at your local library can give you additional suggestions.

- Take your child on a letter hunt when you are outside, in the car, or at the grocery store. Find objects that begin with the letters of the alphabet. Invite your child to point out and name the letters he finds every day.

Math

- Make three-dimensional number cards with your child. Number index cards 1 through 10. Let your child glue on the number of small objects, such as buttons, that correspond to the number on the card.
- Using two foam egg cartons, cut out 20 cups. In 10 cups, write the numbers from 1 to 10 on the bottom of the inside of the cup, using a permanent black marker. In the other 10 cups, draw dots that represent the numbers from 1 to 10. Turn over the cups, placing the numbers and dots facedown, and mix them up. Have your child turn over two cups at a time and try to make matches.
- Using several spoons of various colors, sizes, and materials (wood, metal, plastic), ask your child to tell you how all the spoons are different, and then how they are alike. Have your child group them into categories, such as by color, size, or the material they are made from.

Fine Motor Skills

- Developing fine motor skills is essential for writing readiness. This means working with and manipulating objects with the hands. Working with the hands builds small muscle control needed for writing. You can help your child by providing tools made especially for preschool children: chunky crayons; thick, non-toxic, washable markers; thick, chunky pencils; safety scissors with rounded edges that are both left- and right-handed; modeling clay; and large beads or pasta for stringing and sorting. Give your child plenty of practice using these tools.

- Make lacing cards by drawing a simple design on a piece of poster board or medium-weight cardboard. Use a hole punch to punch holes along the outside of the design. Cut some yarn, thick string, or cord a little longer than you will need to lace the picture. Tie a knot in one end of the thread. Wrap masking tape around the other end to use as a needle. Help your child lace the yarn through the first one, and then let her do the next one. Have your child color or decorate the design.
- Give your child spring-type clothespins. Encourage her to pick up objects, move them to another place, and release them.
- Buy a large notebook for your child to write in. Encourage her to draw pictures and write about the pictures. Although your child's first pictures will look like scribbles, these scribbles are an important first stage in writing and will eventually begin to resemble letters and words.

Gross Motor Skills

- Use balls of all sizes to help your child practice throwing, catching, and kicking.
- Set up a fitness course, indoors and outdoors, for your child. Have your child help create stations for running; hopping on one foot or skipping around obstacles; walking on tiptoe; walking a straight line; jumping over a barrier (no higher than 6 inches); pedaling a bicycle; or throwing, catching, or kicking a ball.
- Fill an old pillowcase with crumpled newspaper, and sew the end closed. In an open area in your home, let your child kick the pillowcase around or through objects.

Art

- Encourage your child to express himself freely when doing art projects. Avoid asking your child what she is drawing. Instead, express your interest in your child's work by saying "Tell me about your picture."
- Provide art experiences for your child by taking him to an art museum or gallery or checking out art books from the library. Ask your child about what he likes about a particular work. Ask him what he thinks may be going on in the work. Avoid going into critical detail about the work. Let your child enjoy the story the artist is telling.
- Keep plenty of art supplies on hand for rainy days or when your child says he is bored. Encourage him to experiment with several media: painting, collage, printmaking, sculpture, etc. Also, teach your child that part of being an artist is cleaning up after oneself and putting all supplies back in their proper places.

Cooking

- Cooking can be a rewarding experience for you and your child. Not only are you spending time with and giving your child an important tool for self-care, but you are also teaching your child how to count, measure, and cooperate; new words; the importance of following directions; the importance of cleanliness; about time and the order of things; and about textures, colors, and shapes.
- Make the cooking experience with your child a total one. Let your child make a picture of ingredients you will need from the grocery store. Let her go to the grocery store with you and pick out the ingredients on the list. Have your child help set up the utensils needed, stir, mix, pour, and shake; this helps with fine motor skills and hand/eye coordination. Let your child help with cleaning up, too.

Thinking Skills

- Ask your child questions that require her to give you more than "yes" or "no" for an answer. For example, "How is applesauce made?"
- Ask your child to repeat a short sentence after you, or say one number and ask your child to repeat it. Then, ask her to repeat two sentences or numbers, then three.
- Make a habit of asking your child to tell you about one or two of her favorite activities during the day.
- Show your child a simple picture. Ask her to look at it carefully. Take away the picture, and ask your child to tell you all the things she remembers.

MAPAA